Praise for *5 Star Service*

'At Boodles customer service is everything. This book is compulsive and compulsory reading for our staff.'
Michael Wainwright, Managing Director, Boodles

'If you want to transform your customers' experience, then 5 Star Service is the place to start. Even if you think you have customer service nailed, Michael can help you be better. This is a brilliant book that everyone ... and I mean everyone, can take something from. Your customers will thank you for it!'
Simon Perkins, Operations Director, Countrywide Estate Agents

'Michael Heppell has such an authentic and effective voice in teaching people to improve lives by providing richer service. He is clear, convincing, and completely on your side at every step along the way.'
Danny Meyer, CEO, Union Square Hospitality Group and author of *Setting the Table*

To Khedidja
You're a star!
Christine

HOW TO DELIVER
EXCEPTIONAL CUSTOMER SERVICE

5 STAR
SERVICE

THIRD EDITION
MICHAEL HEPPELL

PEARSON

Harlow, England • London • New York • Boston • San Francisco • Toronto • Sydney • Auckland • Singapore • Hong Kong
Tokyo • Seoul • Taipei • New Delhi • Cape Town • São Paulo • Mexico City • Madrid • Amsterdam • Munich • Paris • Milan

PEARSON EDUCATION LIMITED
Edinburgh Gate
Harlow CM20 2JE
United Kingdom
Tel: +44 (0)1279 623623
Web: www.pearson.com/uk

First published in Great Britain in 2006 (print)
Second edition published 2010 (print and electronic)
Third edition published 2015 (print and electronic)

© Michael Heppell 2006 (print)
© Hadrian Holdings 2010 (print and electronic)
© Gloop LLP 2015 (print and electronic)

ISBN: 978-1-292-10020-3 (print)
        978-1-292-10022-7 (PDF)
        978-1-292-10021-0 (eText)
        978-1-292-10023-4 (ePub)

British Library Cataloguing-in-Publication Data
A catalogue record for the print edition is available from the British Library

Library of Congress Cataloging-in-Publication Data
A catalog record for the print edition is available from the Library of Congress
Heppell, Michael, author.
  5 star service : how to deliver exceptional customer service / Michael Heppell. —
Third edition.
    pages cm
  ISBN 978-1-292-10020-3
  1. Customer services—Management. 2. Consumer satisfaction. I. Title. II. Title:
Five star service.
  HF5415.5.H424 2015
  658.8'12—dc23
                                2015025853

10 9 8 7 6 5 4 3 2 1
19 18 17 16 15

Cover design by Two Associates
Cartoons by Steve Burke, DECIDE.

Print edition typeset in 10/14 and Photina MT Pro Regular by 76
Print edition printed in Great Britain by Henry Ling Ltd, at the Dorset Press, Dorchester, Dorset

NOTE THAT ANY PAGE CROSS REFERENCES REFER TO THE PRINT EDITION

This book is dedicated to Vanessa Thompson, The Queen of Customer Service.

And you, the customer. Without you there would be no need for five star service.

Contents

Part 1
The psychology of service

Thoughts are things, so getting your thinking straight first makes it easier to get your actions right later.

Part 2
Emotional engineering

Creating an emotional connection with your customer will be more powerful than any special offer, promotion or free gift and considerably less expensive in the long term.

Part 3
Inspiring interactions

At the end of the day, everyone needs to interact with their customers, so make it memorable. And for all the right reasons.

Part 4
Boiler room basics

You can smile, sing and dance all day, but if your basics aren't brilliant, your customers will quickly find someone else who has their own sparkling systems.

Part 5
Navigating the negatives

You will get it wrong, drop the ball and cause some customers distress. Instead of worrying how you got into the crocodile's mouth, you'll learn how to get out of it.

Part 6
Lessons in leadership

To be a service leader you don't have to be the boss, but if you are the boss you'd better be brilliant at service leadership.

Part 7
Business blueprint

Organisations who excel at customer service make more money and save more money. Need I say more?

Introduction

Welcome to the third edition of 5 *Star Service*.

Perhaps an appropriate question might be, 'Why write a second or third edition?' Well, since the first edition was published in 2006, I'm sure you will agree that your customers have become even more demanding. I'm certain you'll also agree that the pressure on you to deliver amazing service has increased and the expectation is that everyone should be better. So here's how I tackled the challenge of creating this latest edition.

Step One was to re-read the original 5 *Star Service* manuscript and take out everything that wasn't as important, didn't work or just felt dated.

Step Two was to continue my research into creating five star service. That was easy; I'm always on the look-out for brilliant examples of customer service. So far I've added 27 new chapters since the first edition and dozens of ideas to help you create your own amazing five star service culture.

Step Three was to focus on making this book as practical as possible. You, like me, will have read many books, become inspired by the ideas and then . . . nothing happens. So I've updated the section on how you can implement the ideas from 5 *Star Service* with a Customer Service Training Programme for your own organisation.

One of the criticisms of the second edition was that it felt a little 'clunky'. Some readers were troubled that the chapters didn't seem to link. My thinking was to write a book that you could pick up, open at any page and just get started. But what do I know? This book is for you.

So I've divided this edition of 5 *Star Service* into seven sections. You can still read the chapters in any order you like, but there's a little more structure this time.

I'd still advise that you start with the Service Star. It's 'standalone' for a reason. Now let me introduce you to the seven sections:

The psychology of service

Some of what you read here might seem obvious common sense. But I'm prepared to bet you don't do all of it. Some of the ideas will be real differentiators for you, and others may give you confirmation, that warm fuzzy feeling of knowing you are already doing some things right.

There are four new chapters in this section, all based on the increasingly changing world of customer service. So why should you take the time to read this section? Because you can implement EVERYTHING you read immediately, and all it will cost you is a little thought, effort and imagination.

Emotional engineering

Every person reading this book has something in common. You're human. Your customers are human. And your service offering is an interaction between one human and another. And that creates a problem.

Humans are a merry mix up of contradictions, sensitive egos, moods, emotions and pre-conceived ideas.

Your job is to ensure that you deliver top class, well-thought out service so that your customer loves you, stays loyal and keeps you in a job.

The Emotional Engineering section gives you a collection of ideas to help you make enough deposits in your customer's Emotional Bank Account that, when you need to, you can take withdrawals – and never go overdrawn.

Inspiring interactions

There are so many occasions where you need to interact brilliantly with your customers that this section could be woven throughout the whole book.

The fact is, many of your communication 'touch points' will leave your customer either bored or bowled over. Get it right, and a simple communication can be an inspiring interaction.

Boiler room basics

What happens behind the scenes? How can you do the basics better? This part of 5 Star Service will help you to plan your process and ensure you have the firm foundations needed to build a service masterpiece.

The Boiler Room isn't the most glamorous part of a business, and working in it isn't always that much fun. But it's an essential part of the operation and when it stops working, everyone suffers.

These Boiler Room Basics are the simple must do's that every organisation with a goal to create five star service must adhere to.

Navigating the negatives

It is going to go wrong. You will drop the ball. Faultless 365 service doesn't exist. So the trick is to be confident you know what to do when it all goes pear-shaped.

It's worth identifying the potential pitfalls before they happen so that you and your team are already prepared.

Lessons in leadership

This chapter is not for your boss. Anyone can be a service leader. It's about your ability to respond and ensure that you inspire others to model your leadership actions.

If you are the boss, there's a whole bunch of ideas that will help you to get the most out of your team in a fun and positive way.

Business blueprint

At the end of the day, and by the end of this book, businesses want to know how to make more money. Even *not for profit* organisations need an income not to make a profit on.

So the 5 *Star Service* Business Blueprint leaves you with some thoughts and ideas on building your service brand, putting ideas into practice and using 5 *Star Service* as an effective training resource in your company.

All in all, this imprint of 5 *Star Service* has turned out to be a bumper edition, packed with ideas, stories, motivation, tools and techniques to help you to master five star service.

Loving service

Everybody loves being on the receiving end of five star service. It makes you feel special, liked and sometimes even loved. And that makes it easier for your customers to both advocate and forgive.

And that's the key. People talk about really great service and really poor service but rarely about what goes on in between. So if you're thinking 'I don't get any complaints' then that's exactly why you must read this book and test out the ideas immediately. Not getting complaints does not mean you're providing great service — it means people just aren't complaining *to you*! And when you think about it, that's pretty scary. How many times have you been unhappy with the service you've been given but didn't bother to mention it? Answers on the back of a football pitch, please. We are in a massively changing world and one of the biggest changes I've noticed is that customers demand more from less, and they don't even tell you!

So who are the customers who are demanding this high level of service? There are two main types of customer: external — that's everyone who isn't part of your organisation — and internal — that's everyone who is. In a nutshell, you can think of your customers as 'anyone who isn't me'. And all of those people deserve five star service.

Why bother with five star service?

It does sound like an awful lot of extra effort to deliver five star service. And is it really necessary? You're probably not a five star hotel. Perhaps your business usually deals with a mid-range clientele, so surely three star service is good enough when they're paying three star prices?

You might work in manufacturing: is five star service really necessary for you? What if you work for the Health Service or one of the many other public-sector organisations, is five star service even relevant to you?

The answer is a resounding YES!

In fact, never before has it been more important for you to learn and apply these techniques if you want to achieve targets, get noticed (be promoted), earn more, achieve more and be an altogether better you.

If it costs little or nothing to do, and gives you a huge head start over the competition, why would you *not* want to thrill and retain your existing customers and attract new ones on the way? Could you ever have too many customers? What an amazing problem to have, so many happy customers that you needed to expand or raise your prices?

The easy way to five star results

So how do you do it? This book is written as an easy read. I'm a very simple person and I believe in simple models, because I believe simple works.

During my studies for the first edition of 5 *Star Service*, I met a researcher who had spent three years looking at a very specific area of customer service and the impact it was having on a particular sector. After three years he had pages of complicated data, wonderful graphs and fabulous flowcharts. The challenge was: the people who paid him a fortune for the study were not using a single one of his ideas. He knew the answers, he had the evidence, but couldn't get people to take action and do the 'stuff'.

My thinking is rather different — if you can't pick up an idea, use it immediately and experience a benefit from it, then it won't be in this book. I'd actually go so far as to say that some of the ideas are so simple you'll wonder why I've even bothered to write about them. And in response I would ask you to check out how frequently you experience these simple service ideas on a regular, consistent basis. I often hear comments like 'That idea you were talking about, I know that already.' My reply is always the same, 'Great that you know it — do you do it?'

The **secret** isn't in the knowing, it's in the **doing**.

This book will have done its job when we move away from the knowing and get down to taking action.

Beware, however, of merely picking out the simple ideas and adding the others to the 'too-hard' list. Just smiling, saying 'please' and 'thank you' and remembering people's names won't be much use if your systems don't support a five star service approach. Great design is always great design; great personal service only exists when you give it your constant unrelenting attention.

How to get the most from this book

You can imagine that writing a book like this, which is designed to appeal to a wide range of people from differing sectors, could be challenging. When I started to put together the ideas, I found myself becoming concerned that some of the ideas, for example a story about a restaurant, might not be suitable for those who work in an office. I spent many hours wondering how to fine-tune the ideas and make them work for every reader until a friend of mine read the first few chapters and said, 'I can use all of those ideas.' She's a primary school headteacher.

The point is, if you think 'differently' you won't look at an example from a hotel and think that because you don't work in a hotel it's not relevant to you. You'll get creative and ask yourself, 'How does this idea apply to me?' That way of thinking will help you to get the most out of this book.

You'll find some chapters are only a few paragraphs long — don't think the number of words relates to the powerfulness of the ideas. Some of those paragraphs have the very best five star service ideas in them and, if you want to get noticed, remembered and referred, they are the ones to apply immediately.

Isn't five star service something that only works when the whole team are on board?

Imagine you've read the book, you're applying the ideas but you have a bunch of people around you who think that five star service is just for fancy hotels and first-class flights. It shouldn't matter to you that you're the only one who's working five star magic. You are the most important person in the world and your personal values will ultimately make a difference to how well you have lived up to the five star standards. Knowing that you did everything you could to create five star service, you'll be able to hold your head high because you did the right thing. You became dis-satisfied with doing a 'good' job and upped the ante.

You might not always know just how much pleasure you have given to people because of your improved level of service, because just as customers rarely complain, unfortunately they also rarely commend. But you will know you made a difference. And that will make a huge difference to your job satisfaction and to your future career.

There are several team exercises where three or four motivated minds will be better than one. But you can also work on an idea yourself and become a service pioneer. You could read this book from cover to cover or just read an idea a day. It's totally your choice. Lots of organisations have had success by investing in several copies for a team and using 5 *Star Service* as a discussion starter or training resource.

I can confidently state that the vast majority of the stories in this book are true because they happened to me. The rest have been checked out as far as is possible and if there's a little poetic licence from those who told me their stories then I'm going to put that down to their enthusiasm.

Imagine you were the subject of one of these stories, what would you want people to embellish when talking about you? Wouldn't it be wonderful to be described in a way that made you feel appreciated? That motivated you to get out there and do it again and again?

5 *Star Service* is designed to help you be the ultimate professional and create magic moments that get you noticed, remembered and referred. Those who embrace 5 *Star Service* walk a different path, and those who don't — don't. So read on, and remember:

Once you've read it, don't just know it — **do it!**

1

The Service Star™

Here's a simple way to measure month by month how well you and your organisation are doing in the five star service stakes.

You can do this exercise as an individual or as a team, and it is a great starting point to see just how well you are doing and where you need to improve. For the first couple of times it's important to follow the instructions carefully but after a while you'll be able to do a spot check in just a few minutes and see how well (or how poorly) you are doing.

This simple diagnostic tool obviously works best when you are completely honest. There's no point in giving the scores you hope for as you won't be able to measure your improvement. Look at it as you would a medical – you wouldn't want the doctor to say you were fine if she'd found something wrong that could easily be fixed. It's the same here:

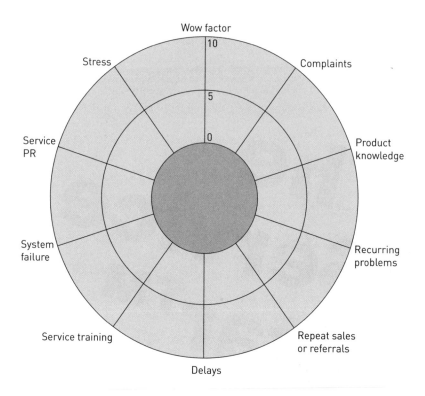

And sometimes the biggest challenges are the most exciting area to conquer first – you just need to know what they are.

You'll score yourself out of 10 for each 'spoke' on the Service Star™. Be careful that you read the description carefully though as in some areas you may actually do well by getting a lower score.

You can score this as an individual, for your whole organisation or just a department. It's up to you, but whichever way you choose, be consistent in your approach.

Step one is easy. Just write today's date on the top left corner. If you don't want to write in your book, or want to do this as a team exercise, you can download more Service Stars™ for free at www.michaelheppell.com.

Wow factor

Do you wow your customers? Are you the type of person who is known for the amazing wows they give their customers every day? Are you the one who always seems to find a way to connect and make their day? Do you turn the complaints into compliments and have a reputation for being able to triumph over disaster? If that's you – you're a 10!

Or do you just get on with it? It's not really anyone's job to wow, we'd rather focus on staying afloat and customer service can be someone else's responsibility. If that's you – you're probably a 1 or a 2.

Or you may find you're somewhere in between. Give yourself a mark.

Complaints

Do you get people complaining about you, your department or your company? I'm talking internally and externally here. Do you complain about other people in your organisation and the service they give you? If you feel like there's a lot of complaining going on then that's a *high* mark, an 8, 9 or even a 10 if you don't think it can get any worse!

Or do complaints happen so rarely that it's almost a unique event? Internally and externally? Are you a special breed where it's hard to complain because there's nothing wrong with you, your systems, your service or your customers? If that's the case then you'll score nice and low on this one. Give yourself a mark.

Product knowledge

So how's your product knowledge? Are you so 'genned up' you could write the manual? You know the history, design and every facet of your product. In fact, you are the 'go to' person when anyone needs more product knowledge. Congratulations, you're a 10.

Or do you know just what you need to know? If you need additional information, you can look it up. After all, it's only a Google search away. Fair enough, but it's mid-marks for you.

Or are you winging it? You haven't got a clue why it does what it does, is what it is or says what it says. After all, it's not your job to know everything. You can't argue with facts, so, if you're just propping up the knowledge table, it's a low mark here I'm afraid.

Recurring problems

Do you nip it in the bud as soon as a problem occurs? Are you the type who looks for a challenge even before it happens and makes sure a brilliant system is in place that removes the problem before it rears its ugly head? If you do, then you're going to score nice and low in this area. If that's really you, give yourself a low mark.

Or do you have the same challenges coming up again and again? In fact you may have some come up so often you've named them! If recurring customer service problems are part of the way you do things then you'll probably score a high mark in this recurring problems area. Give yourself an honest mark somewhere between 0 and 10.

Repeat sales or referrals

Cha-ching, there goes the till with yet another sale, this time from a customer who was referred by a colleague or a friend. Ring ring, there's one of your best customers on the phone making another purchase because they wouldn't dream of going anywhere else. Listen carefully . . . someone is talking about you with such reverence that you are definitely going to get Employee of the Month – again. If that sounds like you then I think you can safely give yourself a high mark for repeat sales and referrals.

Or do you have to battle for every new customer? Work hard on building new relationships by convincing people of your merits? If you aren't being referred and recommended or your customers aren't coming back then it's a low mark this time. Give yourself a score.

Delays

Think for a moment about your customer's experience. How long does it take before someone picks up the phone? Do they get the right person first time? How long do they have to wait for information?

If you're speedy and you do what it takes to cut out the queues then you'll find yourself with a nice low mark here. However, if your delays add up to days and your systems are switched to slow, it may be you'll be scoring yourself high in the delays department.

Don't delay – give yourself a mark.

Service training

An easy one this time. How much time, energy and resources do you put into service training? Are you committed to weekly huddles and monthly training mornings? Do you get the training resources you need and take the time to make them work?

Or do you tend to drift in and out of service training now and then? Are you at the bottom of the pile when it comes to customer service training? I know – you're just too busy!

If you're committing time to learning and applying, give yourself a nice high mark. If you just can't seem to fit it in, I'm not asking for your excuses, just mark yourself appropriately low. Or you may be somewhere in between. You decide and give yourself a mark out of 10.

System failure

How good are the systems you have? Do they smooth the way or trip you up? If you have no systems at all then you may think it's difficult to know whether they're failing or not. Trust me, if you don't have a system, you've failed and that's equal to a high mark for system failure.

The same applies if your system is just too complicated or ambitious. When the right hand doesn't know what the left is doing it means you have a system failure. When a new person has joined your team and after a few weeks they don't know what to do, or how to get the right information, your system has failed. All these outcomes will give you a high mark for system failure.

Or you may have such great systems that failure isn't even considered. It all works perfectly and when you do have a problem you have a system to pick it up and sort it. That would give you a nice low mark for system failure. Give yourself a mark.

Service PR

What's your reputation like? Are you a Ritz Carlton or a British Rail?* Think about what people might say when they talk about you. Are they praising your amazing customer service or are they using you as the example of how not to do it? Worse still, are they just not talking about you at all?

If you're well known for your five star standing and are independently acknowledged for the wonderful way you work, you can safely give yourself a high mark here. Alternatively, if you have a reputation that you think stinks or if you have no reputation at all to speak of, you'll probably need to give yourself a low mark on this spoke.

*British Rail ceased to exist in November 1997 but is still used as the butt of many poor-service jokes.

Stress

Do you feel it? Do you take it home? Is it overwhelming? If you're feeling stressed most days and it affects how you feel physically as well as mentally then I'm afraid it's a high mark.

If you feel stressed on a regular basis, but certainly not all the time, then you might want to give yourself a mid-way mark.

And if you never get stressed, you can take any situation at any time and feel completely relaxed, then you can reward yourself with a nice low mark. And, relax . . .

Finally

Now that you've scored each area, join the dots with simple straight lines. If you're perfect then you should find you have a nice five-point star starting with a 10 'wow factor' running round to a zero for 'service PR'.

Or you may have a mish-mashy lump in the middle or, worse still, you may end up with a 'reverse star' where your point is at the bottom! If so, don't worry – it's your first time and I'm here to help.

There are dozens of ideas on the following pages to transform your lazy lump to a five star Service Star™.

And here's the good news. Get your stars sharp and pointy for five months running and those five stars will be the making of you and your amazing customer service.

The goal – A perfect Service Star™

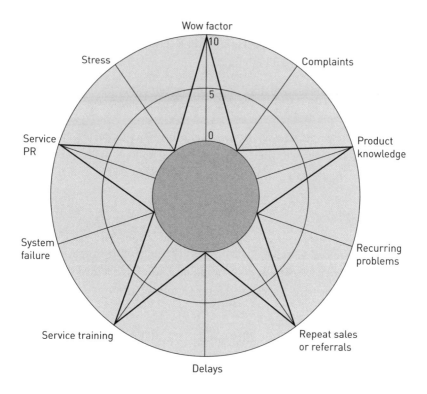

A typical first attempt

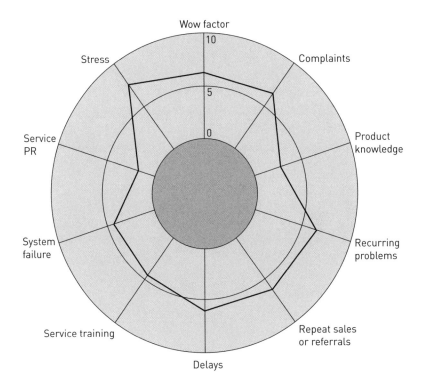

PART 1

The psychology of service

Thoughts are things, so getting your thinking straight first makes it easier to get your actions right later.

2

Loyalty 3.0

I n 1998, **Jeffrey Gitomer published his book**: *Customer Satisfaction is Worthless, Customer Loyalty is Priceless.* I remember reading it and thinking how important loyal customers are and how so many organisations just don't get it.

In the first pages of the book he asks the question, 'Which would you rather have: 1,000 satisfied customers or 1,000 *loyal* customers?'

The obvious answer is both. But given the choice I'd go with loyal. Loyal customers spend more, are your strongest advocates and forgive you when things go wrong.

Everyone talks about loyalty these days. The challenge is: the parameters for loyalty have changed.

Here's where it began.

Loyalty 1.0

The core belief: we do what we say we will do. No big deal really, but when those around you are reneging on their promises, it's a perfect starting point.

It then developed into:

Loyalty 2.0

The core belief: we do what *you* want us to do. Being a customer-driven organisation is tough. Especially as some customers really don't know what they want. That's why organisations who practise building Loyalty 2.0 have more conversations, ask better questions and regularly engage directly with their customers.

These days your customers demand:

Loyalty 3.0

The DNA: we do what you want and we do it better than anybody else possibly could. And we add new dimensions and experiences that you couldn't have even imagined.

By accelerating your service offering beyond what your customers thought they wanted and providing them with more than they thought they needed *then* you create a higher level of loyalty. If loyalty was a software package, this would be Loyalty 3.0.

You can still run Loyalty 1.0 and 2.0 in your company, and I'm sure you'll get results. But why not install 3.0 and really liven up your loyalty?

Obviously, installing Loyalty 3.0 takes a little more than a download and re-start. But the fundamentals of a software upgrade and installing Loyalty 3.0 are the same.

I asked my IT support chaps what was most important when installing new software. They said, 'capacity'. New software invariably takes up more space and requires more processing power.

It's the same if you switch from Loyalty 1.0 to 2.0 or 2.0 to 3.0.

There's no point installing Loyalty 3.0 if you don't have the capacity to implement it.

Next was a good clean-up. Apparently you can delete unused and unwanted files from a computer. I say 'apparently' because I tend to keep everything! Our clever IT chaps work away in the background, deleting unwanted files and features, ensuring our systems run smoothly and generally do whatever it takes to avoid any system failure.

Moving up to Loyalty 3.0 requires a clear-out too. This may be people, systems, brochures, equipment, communication methods and, most importantly, bad/old habits.

But Loyalty 3.0 isn't the finished product. The more you use it the more you'll need patches and upgrades. Loyalty 3.1 will be next. It'll happen quickly and, before you know it, your customers will become so used to this new way of working you'll be looking for the next configuration.

Loyalty 4.0 is coming.

3

Make them feel famous

Imagine you're a county solicitor. You have a small practice with two fellow partners and four support staff. You're a reasonably happy bunch, with your office on the high street and a steady stream of regular customers.

One wet Wednesday morning you notice you have an appointment with a Mr Craig. He's due at 10.30am and would like to talk about conveyancing.

How boring.

Right on time your assistant comes to the door looking rather excited. 'Mr Craig is here to see you.'

'Show him in,' you say with indifference.

And in he walks. But this is no ordinary Mr Craig — it's Mr *Daniel* Craig.

Yes, James freakin' Bond has just walked into *your* office!

He's about to buy a cottage down the road and he's fed up with those 'rip-off lawyers in the city' so he wants to stay local and hopes you can help.

'Would you like some tea or coffee, Mr Craig'? You say.

'Yes, please. Do you have camomile?' He asks.

You don't have camomile. But there's a little Waitrose 50 metres away that someone can dash to, and, to be honest, if he'd asked for a vodka martini — shaken, not stirred — you'd have made it personally.

'Of course, Mr Craig.'

Please answer this honestly. If that were you, would Mr Craig get exactly the same level of service you would normally give? Or do you ramp it up a notch (or 20) for 007?

Last year we presented a 5 *Star Service* day for 200 managers from Mitchells and Butlers. It was one of our favourite events of the year, mainly due to the enthusiastic audience who were right up for both learning and applying loads of ideas from 5 *Star Service*.

Just before lunch, we were exploring the *Emotional Bank Account* and how pubs can make deposits. Sophie Johnson, an enthusiastic business manager, captured the essence of 5 *Star* perfectly when she said, 'We should make our guests feel famous.'

Brilliant!

Even if you don't want to *be* famous, you want to *feel* famous.

We are fortunate to have some friends who are very well known. You would call them celebrities. When we go out with them things change. The service seems to go up a level; staff smile more, they want to engage and there's a tingle of excitement in the air.

We have many more friends who aren't famous. When we go out with them nothing changes. The level of service stays the same; staff smile occasionally, don't really engage and there's not a lot of excitement.

Sophie hit the nail on the head when she suggested we start making customers feel famous. And if you didn't spot it, the key word there is *feel*.

How about this for a staff brainstorm?

What can we do to make our customers feel famous?

Your brainstorm could start with some headings, 'Should do', then move on to 'Could do' and end up with 'Will do'.

And don't give me any of that 'we already do' claptrap.

Even if you do have famous customers, or believe you already treat your customers like stars, take it to the next level. And if you're not impressed with celebrities then treat your customers like a sporting star, a world leader or a Nobel Prize winner.

Test making your customers feel famous for this week and I guarantee, you'll feel the difference.

4

Trust me

Whenever someone says, 'Trust me', I automatically ask them, 'Why?'

Trust cannot be invited — it must be earned.

Brilliant Bikes (brilliantbikes.co.uk) are the kings of cycling service. Their founder, Andrew Page, started his business with a goal to be known as the best customer service cycle shop in the world.

That's a big ambition, but 1,000-plus 5-star Trustpilot reviews would suggest he's done it. I wanted to know what he does that others don't.

I tracked him down in Malmö, Sweden (that's another story) where he was happy to share multiple examples of what he does to build trust with his customers and what one of his key suppliers does to earn his trust.

Although most of Andrew's business is online, he has a small shop in Chobham, Surrey. On many occasions he's fixed a problem or supplied a part and allowed the customer to drop off the payment 'the next time they're passing'. It's one of the nice touches a small shop can do that the bigger ones can't.

But what really impressed me was how he takes things to the next level. From opening early for someone who lived outside of the area to fixing someone's bike on Christmas Eve who was cycling home to his family, he's always on it.

The Christmas Eve customer was fortunate enough to be picked up by Andrew's wife — 50 miles from his destination and with no money. Brilliant Bikes insisted he didn't have to pay — it was an early Christmas present.

Andrew had a challenge at the Post Office. As his business started to grow he would often hold up the queue with multiple packages. He was determined to fulfil his promise of 'First Class Post with no postage costs' but as the orders rolled in, so did the time taken to post them. The postmaster invited Andrew to trust him.

His idea was simple. Leave a stash of cash at the Post Office, drop off your parcels, and when the queue isn't so busy I'll weigh them and guarantee to get them sent the same day.

Perfect. And what do think has happened when there hasn't been enough money to cover the postage? Yes, the postmaster kept his promise and they squared up the next day.

Trust must be earned.
Can I trust you?

Five ways to earn and build trust

1 Never ask for it.

2 Put a big deposit in your customer's Emotional Bank Account.

3 Trust someone with a payment. You might get stung once or twice but in most cases it's worth it.

4 Never judge. What's important to your customer may not be important to you. But right now they think they are the most important person in the world, and, if you can connect with that, you'll undoubtedly earn their trust and loyalty.

5 Always — without exception, excuse or explanation — do what you say you will do.

5

One chance to make a first impression

The **first thing** that many women notice about men is their shoes. For the sake of a couple of minutes you would think more blokes would spend some time giving their footwear a freshen up. I know women who have walked out of restaurants, refused to buy clothes and turned away a rep because they had dirty shoes.

The first thing that most men notice about a woman is her smile (or lack of one). Men generally love a woman who smiles. Not in a sexual way but in a connective way. Most men may never look at a woman's shoes, but they'll always look for a smile.

This doesn't mean that men don't need to smile and women can have dirty shoes. The smile is one of the most important actions you can take, and it's simple.

After shoes and smiles there is a whole range of other impressions we give, often before we've opened our mouths.

Tim Price built Execarel, a successful telecoms company. He loves to meet with sales people (don't all call him at once) and finds it fascinating how poorly most people make a first impression. *Here are Tim Price's top five observations of what not to do:*

1 Wearing what you wear to go out on a Saturday night to work. His basic premise is that you shouldn't try to be trendy for work. Tim points out that you can spend a small fortune on a shirt for a night out that looks great on a dance floor, but the ideal shirt for work should be completely indistinctive. If you don't give people anything to object to then they can't.

2 Colourful socks. I laughed until my sides hurt when Tim recounted a story of a 'big shot' sales executive who came to see him about a massive deal and, after a minute of conversation, crossed his legs and revealed his Homer Simpson musical socks. Classic.

3 Hair gel or over-styling. Again it goes back to the Saturday night vs work look (it's often young men who are the biggest culprits for this one).

4 Bad posture. Slouching, leaning to one side, resting on elbows all put Tim (and probably thousands of others) right off.

5 Bad breath or body odour. Seems very obvious but a packet of mints, a good scrub and some deodorant can go a long way.

I'll add three more which can turn a first impression into a lasting scar for me:

1 A weak (wet fish) handshake. A good firm handshake is essential. They should teach this at school.

2 Being late.

3 Being put on hold without being asked.

Actions

What do *you* think people should or shouldn't do when making a first impression? Write a list of 10 shoulds and shouldn'ts, then do them or don't.

6

Forget about the exceptional

've waited all of my 47 years to experience the Gleneagles Hotel, the legendary Perthshire paradise. In the end I had to go because I was determined to meet hospitality heavyweight Bernard Murphy, and there were no signs that he was planning to come and stay with me.

Bernard is the MD of Gleneagles and he's a service samurai. I knew he would have amazing stories I could retell to inspire super Wow's in the world of customer service.

Over a cup of coffee he was blisteringly honest about the challenges of running such an iconic estate. Then he hit me with an astonishing truth.

I'd just asked him about the Ryder Cup. For non-golfers (like me) it's where Europe's best pitch and putters take on their counterparts from the USA.

It appears to be a big deal.

I know it's a massive global event with TV audiences in the multi-millions, but it still looks like a bunch of blokes whacking little white balls into tiny holes using an assortment of sticks to me.

Gleneagles had a long-held ambition to host the Ryder Cup, and created the Centenary Course in 1993 especially to attract it. Twenty-one years later they achieved their goal.

'You must have put all of your efforts into hosting the Ryder Cup,' I suggested.

'Actually, no,' came the surprise reply from Mr Murphy.

He went on to explain that there was a massive danger in focusing so much on the Ryder Cup that you forgot about your day-to-day business.

Consider that for moment.

Your business works for 20 years to land a major global event, but your advice to your team is to double their efforts on your day-to-day business.

Staging the special event, winning the award, getting the PR, hosting the VIP etc. is sexy, but it can easily get in the way of core, day-to-day service.

Mrs Smith who saves every year for her three-day Gleneagles break with her family couldn't care less if Rory McIlroy is playing Tiger Woods next week.

Get it right for her and she's back next year. And the next. And so are her family.

The Ryder Cup isn't.

The lifetime value of a customer can often be forgotten in the pursuit of something that is (briefly) more exciting.

Day-to-day core business may not be as sexy, but it separates the good from the brilliant.

Here's a challenge. Take a pen and write down the top five day-to-day interactions you have with your customers. From the way you answer the phone to the way you say goodbye, your email style to your method for taking money. Don't stop until you find your top five day-to-day interactions.

Now, ask what would have to happen to make them brilliant? Not just for today or tomorrow but day after day, week after week, year after year — to be consistently brilliant.

7

Big Buyer is watching you

don't know about you but I'm a compulsive eavesdropper. I can't help it! I love to listen in to other people's conversations on the train. I'm fascinated with what's going on behind the scenes in restaurants, shops and hotels and my absolute favourite is earwigging when two members of staff are talking about their company. Isn't yours?

The easy answer is to claim that you would never do such a thing and you respect a person's privacy. But can you honestly tell me that if you were in a shop and you overheard two members of staff criticising their company, you wouldn't hang around for a listen? And then you'd decide whether or not you wanted to hand over your hard-earned cash.

Yes Big Buyer is watching, listening and reading about you.

Out of sight, out of ... mind? Customers are nosy; they love to be in the know and can't wait to catch you out. A dirty backroom or disorganised office will create instant doubt in a customer's mind.

You get only **one chance** to make a **first impression.**

I remember when I first started my business. I had nothing but my enthusiasm. I even had to borrow an old car (with no brakes) to get to appointments. During my first week of trading I set a goal to see 20 new customers. I arrived outside the offices of my first prospect and skipped in to the meeting. I pitched and promised to make them super successful and explained in detail exactly how I'd do that.

After the meeting, as I was getting back into the car (the one with no brakes), I looked up at the office window and was horrified to see the person I'd met with peering out of the window. Through a sarcastic smile he mouthed to me 'nice car' as he pointed at my borrowed wreck.

What kind of image was I portraying? One minute claiming I could make them more successful and minutes later looking like I couldn't even do that for myself! Big Buyer is watching.

If you have any area of your business that you wouldn't want your customers to see then change it, and create an environment you can be proud of.

Customers are listening too. Clients find it rude and disrespectful when staff are having conversations among themselves instead of dealing with their customers' needs. Big Buyer is listening.

And it's never been easier for customers to have a voice through blogs, review websites, instant messaging, social media, etc. You can't stop it, but you can learn from it.

If you're embarrassed by what people say about your organisation online then what are you going to do about it? Whose fault is it when things get out of hand?

Would you want to board a flight if the first image you found when doing a Google search of the potential airline was of drunken staff on a boozy night out? I'd think twice too.

Your customers are watching you. And more closely than you think. Your conversations are overheard, your Facebook pictures are probed and your 'secrets' are common knowledge.

But it's not all bad news. Because customers are more savvy than ever, here are some things you can do to show that you care.

Search Google with your company name followed by 'customer service' or complaint; get past the corporate fluff and read what people are really saying.

Check your 'staff only' areas. Would you be happy for your customers to see them? If you have a kitchen would you be proud to show it off?

If your staff are going to talk about their company, make sure it's positive. What do you want your customers to hear?

If you get negative feedback online don't hide, respond to it.

8

99 per cent
of people
of people
are good ...

... so please don't treat me like the other 1 per cent.

Here's the deal. I'm shopping. Not my favourite pastime: in fact I'm one of those people who loves the idea of getting all my clothes for the year in one fell swoop. Nothing pleases me more than to find an item of clothing that fits well and looks good, then ordering exactly the same in black, blue, brown, grey and six other colours in between.

On a recent excursion to a very well-known store, I had a bundle of stuff that I wanted to try on and I arrived at the changing rooms. The ever-so-efficient assistant announced, 'You can only take a maximum five items into the changing rooms.' Of course I had four times that as I was in shopping mode and stocking up for the winter. Plus I'd be doing anything to avoid coming back. So I had to ask, 'Why?'

'It's a security measure,' she claimed.

'I'm sorry, but I don't feel any more secure by only taking five items into the changing rooms,' was my attempt at a humorous retort.

'No, sir, it's security for the store – to reduce theft.'

At this point she had no idea that by association my subconscious mind had asked, 'Who are you calling a thief?' My conscious mind said, 'I hope she doesn't think I look like a thief!' and my mouth blurted out, 'OK, I'll just take the five at a time.'

But the **damage was done!**

I couldn't try the clothes on in the same way. I didn't feel comfortable in the changing room as I kept looking in the mirror thinking I should be trying on a ski mask or pushing a pair of tights over my head.

You guessed it, I didn't buy a thing. I didn't get past the first five items before waiting until she was distracted and running out of the door. I now have an association with the shop which doesn't really float my boat and according to the news the company is currently 'struggling in an ever more competitive high street'.

Simple message. I hate thieves. I despise the fact that I work hard for my money, pay tax on my earnings, pay tax again when I buy a product, queue at the counter and do everything by the book while other people are just taking stuff without paying. I'm sure you feel the same.

So **don't** make me **feel** like you have the slightest doubt in your mind that **I could be one of them!**

I want to be trusted as a customer. Trust is one of our deepest emotional values. When I'm trusted I feel good – when I feel good I *buy stuff*; when I'm buying stuff you can bet other people are buying stuff too.

Here are some examples of other organisations that trust first:

Self-service checkouts – I know they are cheaper to run but if you have ever used one you'll know you scan everything (usually very carefully) to make sure you get it right and pay for everything.

The person in the shop who, when they see you are a few coins short, asks you to 'just drop it in the next time you're passing'. I bet you have made a point of paying off a tiny amount because someone trusted you.

So what if you work in a place where 'company policy' dictates that 'we can't allow more than five items in the changing room'? How could the lady at the start of this chapter have handled the situation in a five star way?

Just imagine if, as I walked towards her, she had stepped out from behind the desk and said, 'Here, let me help you with those,' then taken some of the items from me. Then if she had added, 'You've got some great clothes here, let me find a changing room for you. OK, sir, our rooms aren't very big so can I suggest you take four or five items at a time and I'll look after the rest. If you want to change anything just give me a shout and I'll bring it through and swap it for you.'

I'd buy the lot!

I don't want to be treated like the 1 per cent. I appreciate in retail it's a challenge that people steal your stuff but if you don't trust me I'm going to be taken down an emotional peg or two and that could make me unhappy. Unhappy people don't buy as much. Unhappy people tell their friends and anyone else who cares to listen about their problems (you could be one of them). Unhappy people really don't buy as much. Unhappy people make your store look gloomy. Oh yes, and in case you didn't pick it up,

Unhappy people buy less, a lot less!

So the next time I'm buying something from you, 'Trust me – I'm a customer!'

Actions

There are three questions to ask yourself:

1 Do you ever say 'it's company policy'?
2 What could you say instead?
3 When might you cause a problem for your good customers by preventing being hurt by the bad?

9

The top three referability habits

A survey was carried out among 1,000 customers which asked them what it would take for them to refer an organisation to their friends or family. One question specifically asked what an individual had to do. The top three answers were:

1 Always **do** what you **say** you are **going to do**.

2 Be on **time**.

3 Always say **please** and **thank you**.

I'm not surprised by the first one. It makes perfect sense that if you are going to promise that something will happen, it's up to you to make sure you deliver the cookie. I remember an old boss of mine once saying, 'We have to under-promise and over-deliver.'

Those days are gone – now you just have to fully *promise and over-deliver.*

In simple terms, *do what you say you're going to do.* People are reluctant to take responsibility as there are a million good reasons why 'what should have happened didn't'. We blame suppliers, we blame technology, we blame colleagues, we blame outside forces and internal politics, but at the end of the day if we're going to create five star service we have to take the responsibility to get things done firmly on the chin. That's why if you bought this book for yourself or if you were given it by somebody else, I would ask you to think, 'What can I get out of the book for me and how can I make a difference to my organisation?' By doing this you'll provide five star service on a consistent and regular basis.

'Be on time' reminds us that if we say we're going to do something by a certain time, we should do it.

Often we think it's a good excuse not to be on time because we are so busy. Actually it's **because people are so busy** that it's more important than ever to **be on time.**

My friend Jeremy Taylor runs his life on what he calls 'Jes time'. He's a busy guy running a very successful business, but he's always on time for every appointment and every meeting. He understands that roads are busier than ever and most things take longer than planned. If he plans his day well he gets masses done, then gets home in time for his wonderful family.

He works it like this. If he has an appointment at 10 o'clock he plans to be there by 9 o'clock. He would rather sit outside for 20 minutes reading his notes and walk in 10 minutes early than arrive 10 minutes late making apologies and moaning about 'the state of the roads', 'the lack of parking' or 'the overrun of his last meeting'. Jeremy gets lots of referrals.

The third referability habit is more puzzling because it has a very specific point which came out of the survey. Not just to be polite but to actually say your Ps and Qs. When I read it I started to take a mental note of how often I remember to say 'please' and 'thank you' and I asked my team and family to point out when I didn't. I was shocked. I would consider myself to be an incredibly polite person but it's only when you stop and look at your actions and omissions that you really realise how many times you forget to say those simple words.

Here's a challenge. For the next 48 hours, when you engage with anyone, be conscious of how many times you do or don't say 'please' and 'thank you'. You may wish to do what I did and ask some of your key people (friends, family, work colleagues) to point out when you forget.

Often it's the small things that make the big difference – see the chapter on *Wee Wows*™ for more.

Actions

Promise *and* deliver. Take responsibility (the ability to respond) seriously. If you say it's going to be done, make sure it happens.

Work on 'Jes time' and plan to get there early. You can do lots with the extra time you have if you should get there early, or if you are running late it's a lovely feeling to have half an hour or so to fall back on.

Ask your friends and colleagues to (politely) point out when you don't say 'please' or 'thank you'. Make sure you say it sincerely.

PART 2

Emotional engineering

Creating an emotional connection with your customer will be more powerful than any special offer, promotion or free gift and considerably less expensive in the long term.

10

The emotional bank account

'm sure you have a bank account and when it's in credit you feel good and when it's overdrawn it's a little more of a concern. You also have an emotional bank account which works in a similar way. When you have received lots of deposits you feel great but when you have experienced too many emotional withdrawals it doesn't feel so good.

Your customers have an emotional bank account too. And when you've made lots of deposits they feel good, remember you (for the right reasons) and recommend you. When you go overdrawn you won't be top of their Christmas card list and you certainly won't have their loyalty.

The challenge is that often we attempt to provide good service to 'get us out of debt'. By then it's too late. The secret is to create lots of small (or large) deposits first, so that when you have to make a withdrawal you won't go into the red.

Here's an example of how an emotional bank account can work for you as a traveller flying on a discounted airline:

You book a cheap flight and save money	**Deposit**
After a short queue the check-in assistant is pleasant	**Deposit**
You're told your luggage is 2 kilos over and you have to pay extra	**Withdrawal**
Security has short queues and you don't get stopped	**Deposit**
The flight is on time	**Big deposit**
Your boarding number is called and the scene is similar to that of a Spanish bull run!	**Withdrawal**
You board the flight and receive a polite, sincere welcome	**Deposit**
Once on the plane you're told that there is a problem with some equipment and you will have to sit on the plane until an engineer can check it out – it takes the next two hours	**Withdrawal**

How the staff handled the first part of your flight experience will make a massive difference to how well you take the news that you have to sit on the tarmac for the next two hours. We've probably all met customers who will do anything to preserve the goodwill of an organisation. Why? Generally because they have had so many deposits made into their emotional bank account by that organisation that they will do anything to defend it.

You've probably done it yourself. Have you ever been in a restaurant and had an absolutely amazing meal so you went back again and again? Then one night you went for a meal and the service wasn't up to scratch, the food wasn't to the usual high standard and the evening could be viewed as a bit of a disappointment? I'd gamble you started to defend the restaurant, especially if you had other people with you. 'It isn't normally like this, maybe they've got some staffing problems,' or 'I hope everything is OK, I noticed that Julian the head waiter isn't in tonight. Next time we'll book when he's here.'

That night the restaurant took some withdrawals from your emotional bank account but because it had made so many deposits beforehand you will go back. In fact, if anybody asks you about the restaurant and whether it's a good place to eat you will completely blank the bad experience from your mind and tell them about previous meals and the fantastic service you get from your friend Julian.

However, if you went back another two or three times and continued to receive the same bad service, low-grade food and poor value for money, it wouldn't be long before it would have taken too many withdrawals and had a negative impact on your emotional account. By then it would be too late. Even if Julian was to come and knock on your door begging for you to come back, you probably wouldn't.

Wee Wow™

You can never put too many deposits into someone's emotional bank account. Who knows, one day you might need to make a huge withdrawal.

Think about your customers, internal and external. How are their emotional bank balances? Time to make a deposit?

Actions

Here are five things that will instantly create deposits in emotional bank accounts.

1 Look happy. Facial expression is one of the easiest but most effective ways to make a deposit or a withdrawal from somebody's emotional bank account.
2 Do what you say you're going to do. It's one of the top three referability habits and not enough people do it.
3 Never blame the customer for anything. If the customer knows they are wrong and you resist the urge to blame them, you'll get double deposits in the emotional bank account.
4 Listen carefully. If you really listen and replay what a customer has said, you will score some rapid deposits. Why? Because most people don't listen and most people want to be heard.
5 Be sincere and engage.

11

Wee Wows™

Often we think that the best way to really look after a customer is to wow them. In this book you'll notice many accounts of going beyond the call of duty to wow a customer.

However, there is something you can do consistently but on a smaller scale. Call them Wee Wows™ (or mini wows, or son of wow). Wee Wows™ are the simple ideas that go a long way to making a big difference in how your customers perceive you. One at a time these Wee Wows are great and will help to keep customers 'on side', but do several together and you'll create something very special that your competition will find difficult to replicate.

Here are 20 Wee Wows™ to get you thinking. Your job is to find 20 more!

1   Never accuse

2   Have a firm handshake

3   Listen carefully

4   Hold the door open

5   Start an email with 'Dear___'

6   Smile

7   Use a person's name

8   Act immediately

9   Make notes

10   Say please and thank you

11   Be positive

12   Check your breath

13   Offer refreshments

14   Create nice smells

15   Have pens that work

16   Handwrite 'Yours sincerely'

17   Hand over items the way the customer wants to receive them

18   Establish initial eye contact

19   Tell the truth

20   Do what you say you will do

OK, so they are just wee, tiny little things, but they make a big difference. Next time you are the customer, be aware of how you react when people do 'Wee Wows™' and how they make you feel.

Often we can't explain why we feel a certain way about our customer experiences, and – guess what? – sometimes your customers can't explain why they feel the way they do about you.

Wee Wows™ get you focused on doing the little things well.

Here's an added bonus from using Wee Wows™. People (friends, family, colleagues, pretty much everyone) will like you a whole lot more. And when people like you, you get better opportunities, you are promoted faster (often you get paid more), you are given the benefit of the doubt and you are followed more readily.

Wee Wows™ Work!

12

What's in a name?

Everything!

I f you use people's names on a consistent basis and really care about that person's name, you could receive rewards beyond anything you could have imagined. It's pretty difficult to get sick of hearing your own name – in fact it's almost impossible.

The two replies to the question I ask below could be directed at anybody, but for the sake of the example the person I called was talking to me, 'Michael' or 'Mr Heppell'.

'Hello, it's Michael Heppell here. I'm calling to ask if you know when my shoes will be ready.'

'Just let me check. They are going to take about three more days, is that OK? Is there anything else I can help you with?'

Or

'Hello, Mr Heppell, thank you for calling. Do you mind if I call you Michael? I'll just check on your shoes right now. (Pause while checking.) OK, Michael, I see it's going to take about three more days, is that OK? Is there anything else I can help you with today?'

You could almost drop in a person's name every other sentence and it wouldn't be too much. Plus, when you use a name, you remember a name. And that's really cool when someone remembers your name and you weren't expecting it. (See 'Putting on the Ritz' on page 77.)

But what if you don't have to speak it, you just have to write it? I get my surname misspelt all the time. Heppel, Hepple, Heppal, even Apple are some of the favourites. I love it when someone asks, 'How do you spell your surname, Mr Heppell?', then reads it back to me.

As we are living in a multi-cultural society we are experiencing a wave of new names and spellings into our vocabulary. Most people don't mind if you ask for a pronunciation of their name or a spelling. If I hear a name for the first time I ask, 'Where does that name come from?' and 'What does it mean?' If a person has gone to the trouble of finding out what their name means then, trust me, they love to tell you.

As it happens, most people don't offer you their name. Make it your mission to find out. I make a conscious effort to find out the names of personal assistants, and I work hard to be genuinely interested in them.

People feel insincerity, so if you aren't genuinely interested don't try to fake it – you'll get found out.

Here's a typical call. 'Hi, Wendy, how are you today? Still as busy as ever?' Then as soon as I get a reply I use their name again. 'Wendy, I was wondering, is it possible to get an appointment with Sue at some point early next week? I know she's busy, Wendy, but if anybody can get me half an hour it's got to be you.'

I always make a conscious effort to use names when I'm looking for five star service for myself too. I know that people treat their friends better than they treat strangers, and we tend to call our friends by name.

I don't know about you, but I love going to those events where everyone is wearing a name badge. However, it still amazes me how many people don't actually read the name of the person they're talking to. You don't even have to have a good memory and you can glance, pick up someone's name and be using it within a few minutes. Easy.

Companies often have their directory online which lists the names of all the people you might want to talk to. So when you call you can ask for someone by name – it's much more powerful to ask for someone by name and get the right person than it is to ask for a title or department.

There is no **sweeter sound** for someone than the sound of **their own name** – so use it.

Actions

Two simple ideas for learning and remembering someone's name when you first meet or speak to them:

1 Use repetition and say their name at least three times in the first few minutes. By saying it three times you are 60 per cent more likely to remember it. Say it several times in your head too, that also helps.

2 Create a visual image that links their name to a prominent part of their appearance. The more bizarre the better for this as your brain loves colour, humour and the unusual. So, for example, if you meet someone called Peter Green and he's wearing a big coat, imagine a bright green 'pea' that creates a 'tear' in his coat. Bizarre, I know, but at the end of this book I bet you remember Peter Green before you remember any other names mentioned.

Wee Wow™

Find out the meaning of the 10 most popular names and use this information in conversation. It's a nice idea to have them written down and available if you use the phone a lot.

13

Customer magic moments

Customers need to have **their** magic moments too.

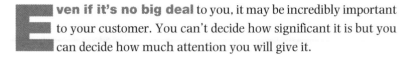

ven if it's no big deal to you, it may be incredibly important to your customer. You can't decide how significant it is but you can decide how much attention you will give it.

I was waiting to meet a client in an overly expensive London hotel when an American lady came through the front door gushing over her new discovery. She grabbed the concierge and proceeded to tell him how a wrong turn became a fortuitous mistake. This is what I heard.

'Can you believe it; I took a wrong turn on the way back to the hotel and ended up in the middle of nowhere!'

The concierge didn't do anything to hide the look on his face which screamed, it's unlikely you could end up in the middle of nowhere in central London.

The guest continued, 'But I'm so glad I did get lost because I discovered an amazing little park.' She pulled out her map and said, 'Look it's right here!'

Now at this point the concierge could have said 50 different things but what he came out with astounded me. He looked at her map and said, 'I know, I walk past there every day.'

Instantly the excited guest looked forlorn. He'd burst her bubble and taken her moment.

So what could he have said? How about, 'Let me see ... wow, what a gem, and so close to the hotel! I walk to work that way, I'll have a closer look tomorrow. Thank you.'

Then can you imagine how the guest might have felt if the next day she had a note in her room thanking her for the recommendation and adding he had followed her instructions and taken a walk past the park that very morning.

I continued to watch this concierge for the next 15 minutes while he recommended routes, booked tables, gave advice on opening times and offered the low-down on the hot spots in town. All of which made him look good, polished his ego and made him feel fantastic. Shame he couldn't do the same for his customer.

Debbie Homer-Davies runs Baby Lady near Canterbury, Kent, which supplies everything a new parent might need — from potties to prams.

First-time parenting is an interesting adventure. Your mobile phone becomes a photo album, every car journey requires meticulous organisation, and if you discover something that might be useful to other mums you can't wait to share it.

Debbie is a huge fan of 5 *Star Service* and used the ideas from my book in her business. I asked for one example of customer 'Magic Moments' and she gave me dozens. Here's one of my favourites.

Baby Lady stocks a very popular toy called a 'Winkel' which lots of customers rave about; 'Did you know if you put it in the fridge it cools really quickly and it's great for baby when she's teething?'

Debbie has undoubtedly heard that same comment lots of times, and if she responded with, 'Yes, lots of mums have said that', then she would be like most other retailers.

But here's what she says instead, 'Thank you, that's a great idea.'

The smiling customer might follow up with, 'I only found out by accident.'

'Thank you for telling me. We'll recommend that to other mums as they're sure to find that helpful. Would you mind if I put that idea in our newsletter?'

A now thrilled mum feels valued, listened to and believes they have made a difference.

Here are the five star ways to make your customers feel magic.

1   Remember, even if you've heard the story a hundred times, it's your customer's first time.

2   Actively listen. Nod, ask questions and make the moment real.

3 Follow up. Add something to make them feel even better the next time you see or talk to them.

4 Share with others what you have gleaned from your customer and credit the source.

5 Be in the moment. Easier said than done. This means you are 100 per cent focused on them. Not checking emails while on the phone. Not looking over someone's shoulder. Not planning what you are going to do next or replaying what's just happened. It means you are there for them and in their moment.

14

What's in a smile?

From just a few weeks after birth, we demonstrate that we feel happy by smiling. All through our lives and until our dying day we use the same process. People are even heard to comment that they'd like to die with a smile on their face.

So take a look around. If smiling is so important, why aren't more people doing it? The next time you walk down the street check out how many people are smiling. You won't be surprised to find that it's often a small minority who find something to smile about. Even when there's good news, people often don't smile.

In these days of high competition, where price and speed crash headlong with convenience and perceptions painted by the media, one of the purest things we can do is to offer a sincere smile.

A **smile** is timeless.

A true smile, one that resonates from the heart, can lift a person and completely change the way they feel. A smile is directly linked to your internal physiology. In other words, when you smile, you connect with your entire nervous system and your whole body reacts in a different way from when you're not smiling.

You have probably read or heard that it takes 17 muscles to smile and 43 to frown (or similar). The truth is it actually takes 12 muscles to smile and just 11 to frown. Here's the breakdown for you facial muscle freaks out there.

Muscles involved in a 'zygomatic' (genuine) smile: *zygomaticus major* and *minor*, which is four. *Orbicularis oculi* – that's two. *Levator labii superioris* – two again. *Levator anguli oris*, which also helps lift the angle of the mouth – two more. And your *risorius* which pulls the corners of your mouth to the side. Again two of these are needed or your smile is one-sided so that gives a total of 12.

And here are the muscles needed to frown: *orbicularis oculi* (again), that's two. *Platysma* – another two. *Corrugator supercilii* (bilateral) and *procerus* (unilateral) gives you a furrowed brow so that's three.

Orbicularis oris, that's another unilateral so there's just one. *Mentalis* is another single so again just one and finally good old depressor *anguli oris* which pulls down the corner of your mouth, two there, giving a frowning total of 11.

But it's only one muscle less, so resist the temptation!

Anatomy aside, don't people prefer smiles? As customer service professionals there has never been a more important time to learn how to smile.

In the movie *Win a Date with Tad Hamilton* the female star, Rosalee, has been loved her whole life by the person she thinks of as her best friend. He knows so much about her that he can describe her 'six different smiles'.

'One when something flat out makes her laugh. One when she's laughing out of politeness. There's one when she makes plans. One when she makes fun of herself. One when she's uncomfortable. And one when ... one when she's talking about her friends.'

Guess what's coming next? What are your six smiles when you deal with your customers? One when they first walk through the door. One when you're on the telephone. One when you're explaining your product. One when you're listening to a story they are telling. One when you're thanking them for their business. And one when you're asking for referrals.

Stop! Wait a minute. I've seen people who smile all the time and look so fake that you don't trust them. *That's why a smile has to come from the heart and be sincere.*

So, what about the smile you use just because you are genuinely happy? When somebody smiles sincerely, you can see it in their eyes. The best way to practise smiling sincerely is to find some sincere things to smile about. Look at things that make you happy and when you feel a smile on the inside, show it on the outside too. If you're near a mirror take a moment to have a look at what you do when you smile sincerely. By having an awareness of how and when you smile, and by practising finding things to smile about on the outside, you'll find it easier and easier to smile sincerely, every day.

The **shortest distance** between two people is a **smile.**

15

Send cards

Did you know that the average person receives fewer than four cards each year for their birthday? Did you know that the average person receives fewer than 10 cards a year for all other occasions? Did you know that the average customer receives *no cards* from their suppliers – ever.

We post them bills, we send them contracts, if we do despatch cards they tend to be mass-produced corporate Christmas cards with a pre-printed message. We rarely send customers cards for anything else. Yet sending cards is a great way to show people that you really care. It's a small action with a massive value. They can be sent to internal and external customers with equally brilliant results.

I once worked with a division of HSBC bank on a project, part of which involved a campaign to send every single member of staff a thank-you card to show how much they were appreciated. When you work for one of the biggest companies in the world it's easy to forget what an important part you play. There are thousands of staff in the division so we needed to devise a method to produce a personalised card. Here's how we did it.

We had a branded card designed and produced (blank inside leaving plenty of space to write a personalised message). The divisional general

manager personally bought all the cards for 10p each and donated the money to the HSBC charity fund. She kept a batch of cards for her own use, then sold boxes of cards to her area directors for 20p each and again all the money collected was donated to the charity. They then kept their own batch and sold the rest to their managers and team leaders. On the back of each card we had a statement printed: 'Sold up to three times for charity.'

Then in the next 30 days the leaders had to find a way to thank their staff, sending them a personal card with a handwritten message. Everyone knew they would receive a card, but they didn't know what for or when. After 30 days there were cards everywhere and everyone had a personal 'feel good' moment (in fact most people kept their cards for months afterwards).

The real people to benefit were the customers. Because happy staff, who are recognised for the good work they do, are better at customer service.

Note to managers – **treat your staff the way** you want them to **treat your customers**.

So what could you send cards to your customers for?

Birthdays

Paying a bill on time

Being patient

For a referral

For a great meeting

For an anniversary

For Christmas

To celebrate their success

As part of an apology

Bonus Bit

Here's a tip on how to make the card even more special.

As well as handwriting the inside, handwrite the envelope and put a live stamp on it (don't use the franking machine).

Think about it: If you get a card in the post with a handwritten envelope and a live stamp among a whole heap of other mail, which are you most excited about opening?

Other ideas around the card theme
Flip chart thanks

If you have a small team, take a bunch of coloured pens and a flip chart pad. Do a page of 'thank yous' using colour, space and imagination for each person in your team. Stay behind late and stick a personal page on an individual's desk, their workstation or on the wall. Arrive slightly later the next morning.

Tweet thanks

As Twitter becomes an increasingly popular way to let people know your thoughts online, perhaps a tweet thank-you may be suitable. Make it even more personal with a link to the person's website.

Send a letter

With the advent of email we don't send as many letters as we used to. If you don't like the idea of a card, a nice letter could make someone's day. When writing a letter, it's a nice touch to handwrite the 'Dear' at the start and it's a must to handwrite the 'Yours sincerely' at the bottom.

Photo thanks

After a successful meeting we'll often get back to our office and write a thank-you message on a flip chart, stand next to the message and have a digital photograph taken. We email the picture to the person we've just met with – they love it!

16

Special requirements

My wife is lactose intolerant. Basically this means that if she eats anything with cow's milk, cream, cheese, yoghurt, etc. she's violently ill for several days.

Unfortunately, if you don't know anyone who suffers from this intolerance or you aren't aware of the effects after an accidental mouthful of the dreadful dairy, then you may just think she has a fussy food fad or is testing out the latest Hollywood diet. She's not.

So you can imagine what it's like for us ordering in a restaurant. 'May I just check, does that have any dairy in it, please? I'm lactose intolerant and can't have any dairy products,' asks Christine.

'I don't think so,' replies the waiter and the order is placed. Our dinner arrives. Christine toys with her potato, then asks the waiter, 'Are you sure there's no dairy in this?'

The waiter then takes a huffy strop, goes back into the kitchen, struts back to the table and announces, 'Chef says there's a tiny bit of cream in the potato.'

That's like saying to a vegetarian, 'There's only a small amount of beef in your meat-free mushroom risotto.' A 'tiny bit' of cream once gave Christine three days of agony.

Here's the flip side. The Rubens Hotel in London knew Christine had a challenge with lactose (a sister hotel in their group let them know – brilliant!). We were staying only one night but became instant fans when we checked in to our room and found two room service menus. The standard one and a second one, marked up by the chef, with all the lovely food Christine could have. We were going to eat out that night but, guess what? Yes, we stayed in and ordered room service.

When your customer has a special requirement you have a choice. You can moan about it, try to placate them and give them your second best option.

Or you can **wow them** by providing a brilliant personal

service, show that you really **understand** their needs and **create a fan** who will talk about how **amazing you are** to anyone with ears!

And it isn't just food. Some people may want to meet you early in the morning, others late at night. For some it might be religious views, which you may not understand but are central to their way of life. Many people have disabilities, some very slight, but they still deserve your consideration.

And if you're not sure what a person's requirements are or how you can help them, then ask. I've yet to meet a person who has a special requirement who minds being asked about it. No matter how obvious it seems.

Finally use a 'heads up' approach (see Chapter 42) and be aware of the less obvious times when someone may need help. Large-print price lists, different language answers to commonly asked questions, a brief understanding of other cultures and an awareness of your environment and how it may affect others can sometimes be the small thing that makes a massive difference.

17

Putting on the Ritz

travel a lot. I was once away from home on business for 130 nights in a year. I didn't stay in the same hotel for longer than two consecutive nights. When you're away so much you become an instant judge of hotels. I know it's not fair to make judgements based on a first impression but hey, we all do it.

Your business might be very different from a hotel, but the two experiences I pick out here perfectly illustrate how the low-cost details make *all* the difference to the customer.

First, the horrendous one.

Glasgow is one of my favourite cities. I lived there for two years and I love the place and the people, so I was really looking forward to going back.

I'd been on the road for 10 days doing lots of speaking and training engagements and arrived at my hotel at 5.30pm. It was a big city-centre hotel with an impressive foyer. A queue of about 20 people was stretched across it waiting to check in – and only one person was on the front desk. After a few minutes I started to look down the line, hoping another person would join the receptionist. They didn't. After a further 45 minutes it was my turn. I walked to the desk, started to say a nice hello and the receptionist didn't even look up. In fact, as I started to speak she put up her hand to stop me and when she was ready she looked up. Not the best start.

She looked me up and down (I had two cases, a rucksack and computer bag) and she said only two words, 'Checking in?'

'No, I'm here for a colonic,' I found myself saying. Quickly followed by, 'Yes, actually I am.' She had a look on her face which in a nanosecond revealed that colonic hydrotherapy was not high on her list of priorities and she was in no mood to be dealing with the likes of me.

'Name?' That was her next attempt at engaging me. Now I have a surname that can be spelled in several ways, so I always say it, then spell it to help. 'It's Michael Heppell. And Heppell is spelt H. E. P. P. E. L. L.'

She then tapped something into her computer which I know wasn't Heppell, because with great pride she looked up from her keyboard and announced,

'You're not on the system.'

'I should be on the system,' I replied, beginning to regret the joke about the colonic. 'I've got a booking reference and confirmation.'

'Get me the number,' was the affectionate reply.

It took me a further five minutes to put my bags down, find my travel file, locate the booking reference number and read the 28 digits, letters, back slashes and hyphens to her. Then she looked at me, rolled her eyes, and said, 'Oh you meant "Heppell".'

She then asked me to fill in my home address, nationality, etc. on the card (passed to me upside down) and to sign next to the two crosses. Then she asked me for a credit card. Have you ever been in that situation where you can't get your cards, wallet or purse out fast enough and it just seems to get wedged as you pull? My cards got stuck at a funny angle in my pocket and the more I tried to pull, the more jammed they became. She repeated in a very impatient tone, 'I said I need a major credit card.' Eventually the cards came free and I handed her some plastic. She literally snatched the card from me, swiped it and slapped it down on the desk with an attitude that screamed,

'We do that just in case you **steal the furniture.**'

Then, as if by magic, she suddenly perked up. A big fake smile appeared (must have done customer service training level 2, this one) and rhymed, 'Would you like a wake-up call or a newspaper? Breakfast is served from seven to nine thirty in the restaurant. Enjoy your stay.'

I jumped into the lift and went up to my room. Dropped my cases and had the usual glance around. Then I was really wowed. I went into the bathroom and noticed that they had folded the end of the toilet roll into a little 'v'. Now I was impressed. I felt like calling home and telling my wife that she had to drop what she was doing and make her way to Glasgow as I'd found a hotel that really knows how to 'wow' a customer as they fold the toilet paper into a little 'v'!

Of course, what I was really doing was wondering why they bother with the traditional 'v' in the loo roll (I know every hotel on the planet does it) when they don't seem to spend as much time working on the very first impression a customer has of the hotel – the staff.

I have had worse experiences, but this was a very expensive hotel with a big brand name and a lot to lose. It's kind of stuck with me and I tell the story a lot.

How could they do better?

Here's my favourite example of how to greet a customer.

In 1997 I visited Singapore and had the privilege of staying in the Ritz Carlton Hotel. I made a promise that one day I would revisit and take my family – it really is a stunning hotel.

In 2004 I was doing some work in Australia and Singapore and it overlapped with the Easter holidays. My son was on his gap year in Oz so we decided to combine the work trip with a holiday. After a long flight to Singapore we arrived at Changi airport where I had arranged for a car to pick us up. The driver was polite and suggested we relax for the short journey to the hotel. Within 30 minutes we pulled up at the front of the hotel – and that's when the magic really began.

It had been seven years since I'd stayed at the hotel and, when the door of the car was opened, the beaming smile of the doorman was followed with a sentence that truly sums up five star service. 'Welcome back to the Ritz Carlton, Mr Heppell.' *Seven years!* Yes, seven years since I'd stayed there and the first words I heard were 'Welcome back to the Ritz Carlton'. My wife Christine stepped out of the car after me (remember, this is her first visit) and was greeted with, 'Welcome to the Ritz Carlton, Mrs Heppell. I believe this is your first visit, enjoy your stay.' And as my 11-year-old daughter followed she was greeted with, 'And you must be Miss Sarah, we have a present for you,' and one of the concierge team handed Sarah a small bouquet of flowers.

If it had ended there it would have been great – but it didn't. It just got better and better.

As we walked to reception two members of staff who were walking the opposite way greeted us by name and said how happy they were to have me back and expressed how much they hoped Christine and Sarah would enjoy their stay.

At reception our registration card was waiting for us, printed and completed (with our home address pre-printed on it). It was on the desk, the right way round with a nice pen. All I had to do was sign. *But* – and it's a big but – the receptionist still had to ask me for my credit card. I know that most people reading this book don't work in hotels and many of you will never ask anyone for their credit card, but just learn from this amazing example of five star service from a teenager working as a receptionist. This is what she said after I had signed the registration card.

'Mr and Mrs Heppell, you are going to be staying with us for the next five nights. During your stay you may wish to order room service or perhaps have a drink from the bar. You may wish to purchase something from one of our boutiques or join us for a meal in one of our fine dining restaurants. Perhaps it would be convenient for you to allow me to take a swipe of your credit card so you don't have to worry about carrying money.'

Perfect, perfect, perfect.

What did it cost? The attitude is free. The training costs some initial effort but lasts a lifetime. The system that allows the doorman access to your name after seven years is genius but relies on basic technology. All in all, it's the choice of how you want to treat people.

Does it pay off? I've told this story to audiences all over the world, to FTSE 100 business executives, Fortune 500 leaders. I tell the story on almost every course I teach, certainly at most keynote presentations and pretty much to anyone else who will listen – literally tens of thousands of people from all walks of life.

Many have emailed me to tell me of their experiences and how they went to the Ritz Carlton because I recommended it to them. I never recommend anything formally, I just tell a story.

People are telling stories about you – but rarely TO you.

Does your story have a happy ending?

Update

I haven't been to the Ritz Carlton in Singapore for many years, but I have been to the Chesterfield Hotel in London several times. One night my wife and I arrived at the Chesterfield at around 8pm. The receptionist greeted us with a warm, 'Welcome to the Chesterfield, Mr and Mrs Heppell,' before we checked in with minimal fuss and plenty of warmth. When we got to our room I checked my emails and was surprised to find one from my PA who asked if I had made the reservation for the Chesterfield as she hadn't. After a moment of confusion it dawned on me that we weren't actually booked in!

I went back to hotel reception and asked if we had a reservation for that evening. We didn't but here's where the receptionist shone. After her welcome, she checked their system and, even though we didn't have a reservation, she still checked us in, quickly reviewed our history and put us in a room where we had stayed previously and had commented that we'd enjoyed.

She told me that she didn't think I would want to hear the words, 'You don't have a reservation,' as that may have been embarrassing, so simply made us feel good with no fuss and a perfect execution of efficiency and modesty.

18

Creativity gives better service

Five star service is not always costly. Simple creativity (on a one star budget) can bring affordable but stunning results. Here are a few brilliant examples.

One of my wife's favourite films is *Pretty Woman*. If you are one of the three people in the world who hasn't seen it, much of it is set in a suite at the Beverly Wilshire Hotel, Los Angeles. The Beverly Wilshire has been voted one of the best hotels in the world. It is also one of the most creative, mixing elegant style with some really cool ideas.

Having watched the film for the hundredth time, I promised my family we would visit the *Pretty Woman* hotel and, during a trip to America, we found an opportunity to visit the West Coast for a few days. Only one slight challenge. If you want to relive the *Pretty Woman* experience and take a suite at the Beverly Wilshire Hotel, ideally you'd arrive as a couple. But we love travelling with our kids, so what to do?

Well, the Beverly Wilshire are aware that lots of people want to visit the hotel because of the film (and some come equipped with their kids). So they catered for everyone with a package called 'Not Just the Two of Us'. It was brilliant! Mum and Dad got the fabulous suite with the champagne and strawberries, and the kids got an adjoining room. But even better than that, the kid's room was filled with sweets, 'soda' and ice cream, free movies and a selection of games.

Then there are the outings. The Concierge asked our kids what they wanted to do first and then asked us (the parents who were paying). He then combined everyone's requests and came up with a perfect schedule. Christine and I wanted to do a nosey 'Stars Homes' tour. The Concierge asked us all to make a list of our favourite stars, then he looked at the various tours to see which one fitted best. Typically, no tours featured our requirements so he arranged a private tour. Then he gave the tour company our list so they could work out a route in advance.

On our flight home we were discussing our favourite parts of our trip and we all talked about the *experiences*, not just the rooms, food, tours, etc.

Our best experiences happened when someone considered what would make our time more memorable.

Could you create service solutions to do the same for your customers?

Here's an example from a less glamorous setting. Cheryl Black is a Customer Service Queen, and, pre-retirement she was Customer Services Director with O2 and prior to that Scottish Water, Orange and NTL.

Long before Netflix and other streaming services, NTL (now Virgin Media) enabled people to subscribe to individual movies via its cable connection. This was ambitious new technology and many customers experienced teething problems.

Subscribers would call up and say they had ordered a movie and then been unable to retrieve it. Of course they were entitled to a refund, and as an act of goodwill NTL would offer a free movie on another night.

That was fine, but if the customer's Saturday night had been ruined because the movie wasn't available, they were justifiably disappointed. NTL needed to take it to the next level.

Here's what they did and it made a significant difference. If there was a challenge with the delivery of a movie and a customer called to complain, they would resolve the problem and then ask, 'Do you prefer Chinese or Indian food?' After their response, the Customer Service Adviser would say, 'The next time you watch a movie, we'd like to pay for your take-away. You order a curry and we'll put a credit on your account now to pay for it.'

What a brilliant solution. Recognising that what the customer was really upset about wasn't just about missing the movie, more a ruined Saturday night in. This led them to devise a more appropriate response: not just a credit on a bill, but an even better Saturday night in the next week! They called it 'Making the emotional connection'.

Think about it, it's a win—win and it achieves several things:

1   The problem is solved but they go the extra mile.

2   They add value in more than just a financial sense.

3   They encourage you to watch more movies.

4   They make you feel good. Very good.

Another example comes from a holiday-maker and a Spanish karaoke bar. During one of our *5 Star Service* workshops we heard this wonderful story from one of our participants, Danny.

Danny and his family were on holiday in Spain and on their first night they found a nice local bar with karaoke. Danny loved to sing and quickly wowed the crowd. The owner commented on his enthusiasm and talent and bought him a drink.

The next night they visited the bar again. And again the following night. Danny told the Manager they were going to visit some other bars but they would be back at the end of the week. On their last day, walking back to the hotel from the beach, they saw a sign outside the karaoke bar which read,

'Tonight, and for one night only — Danny.'

Danny was delighted. Not only did he take his family along, he also took another 25 new friends he'd made at their hotel.

Actions

Here are five ideas to get your creative juices flowing:

1 Think like a customer — literally. See how far you can progress through your processes as a customer. Ask yourself what you could do better.

2 Have a brainstorm, but do it properly. You know the rules by now for brainstorming: no negative comments and every idea counts.

3 Next time you have a service issue, ask yourself how nature would deal with it. Nature has a great way of adapting to situations. How would nature deal with your service to make it even better?

4 Free up creativity in others. If you are a manager, allow your teams to think of creative ways to improve your customer service experience.

5 Ask 'What if?' questions. It's a great way to start thinking differently. Here are a few suggestions to get you started. What if:

> we gave away our products for free?
>
> our best customer was going to leave?
>
> I had all the time in the world?
>
> we doubled our budget?
>
> a member of the Royal Family was coming to visit?
>
> we were entering a competition for a Customer Service award?

PART 3

Inspiring interactions

At the end of the day, everyone needs to interact with their customers, so make it memorable. And for all the right reasons.

19

Beware the silent customer

We are in a changing world. Massive changes are taking place every day in technology, ways of working and tastes. However, I really do believe that the biggest change is that

Customers expect more from less *but they don't tell you*!

Yes, expectations are at an all-time high, we are more demanding than ever, but think about yourself as a customer: do you bother to take time to tell people exactly what you want? My guess is a resounding NO! We just don't have the time.

I was travelling recently with a friend of mine who had a real challenge with his hotel room. When he arrived the room wasn't made up; when he eventually went to his room he found he'd been assigned a twin smoking room. He had booked a double non-smoking one. His shower was represented by a faint trickle and the heat from the air conditioning was stifling, with no obvious way of turning it down.

We met in reception and he told me all the problems with his room and 'the nightmare' he'd just experienced. Thirty seconds later the duty manager appeared and asked us whether everything was OK. I looked towards my friend and was amazed when he replied, 'Fine, thanks.'

'Fine! What's fine about it?' I asked once the manager had moved on.

'Oh, I can't be bothered. I'll just make sure I don't come back,' he replied with certainty.

So in this situation, as the manager is thinking everybody's happy, the customers are thinking, 'Make sure we don't book here again!'

Even when we left the hotel and we had the customary customer satisfaction form to fill in, my friend still didn't express his dissatisfaction.

So, how do you know what your customers think about you? **Just**

because they are silent doesn't mean they are happy.

What can you do?

1 Create an environment where people feel comfortable giving you feedback – good or bad. You can do this by being open and honest with people right from the start.

2 Ask power questions that are designed to make people share how they really feel. You can do this by asking, 'What can we do better?' Most people will say, 'Erm, nothing.' Because you are now aware of the terror of the silent customer you can say, 'Thank you. If there was one thing, what would it be?' Then you need to listen.

3 When you ask someone to fill in a feedback card, use these words, 'Would you mind completing a feedback card? Please be as honest as you can because we love feedback, it's what makes us better.'

If you do get a customer who complains, remember to thank them. If you think about it, they are probably speaking on behalf of a couple of dozen other customers who thought it but didn't say it. Then use one of the 50 or so ideas in this book designed to make sure you win them over and keep them for a lifetime of loyalty.

Bonus Bit

Make a list of everything you think your customers want, then the next time you meet with them (or a representation of them) show them the list and ask whether you've got it right and then ask whether they would like to add anything else.

You may think this is a bit cheesy and you may be right, but think what you would do if one of your suppliers did that for you. Imagine how you would feel if the next time you went to your dentist a friendly member of staff took five minutes to ask you to look at a list of potential improvements to service and offered you an opportunity to add to the list. Then imagine how it would feel if the next time you went there they'd applied some of your ideas.

20
super
scripts

Remember the great treatment I received from the receptionist who took my credit card at the Ritz Carlton in Singapore? If you don't, here's a reminder.

'Mr and Mrs Heppell, you are going to be staying with us for the next five nights. During your stay you may wish to order room service or perhaps have a drink from the bar. You may wish to purchase something from one of our boutiques or join us for a meal in one of our fine dining restaurants. Perhaps it would be convenient for you to allow me to take a swipe of your credit card so you don't have to worry about carrying money.'

I don't know how many times a day she says that, but I do know it's a fantastic script. She may vary the odd word or two but basically she says that because it works.

The pros and cons of scripts

You say the right thing, you say it effortlessly and in most cases you know what the results will be.

Scripts give continuity. Great to take a person from A to B. Scripts give confidence. 'I didn't know what to say so I just said nothing' was what one person told her boss recently.

And for those of you who think scripts take away passion, think about watching a Shakespeare play … passionate?

But be careful. How many times have you heard a script delivered in a monotone from a person who, if they weren't standing in front of you, you would swear was reading from a screen? (In lots of call centres they do!) Just because we can't see someone on the phone doesn't mean we can't feel them (see 'Telephone service' on page 101).

Scripts make customer service easier when they are delivered **passionately** and **sincerely.**

Scripts can kill creativity. If you are using a script and you need to digress from it to say the right thing for your company and the customer, then *go for it*. Even the best script can be improved to get the most out of a situation.

The following is an example of where a script works brilliantly. Just imagine you have booked a holiday and the travel agent says to you:

> 'In the next couple of weeks you'll be receiving your tickets followed by final confirmation of your flight times about two weeks before you fly. This is my card and there's my number if you need anything.'

That would be nice. Or what if they said:

> 'Well that's you all set. In the next couple of weeks you'll be receiving your tickets, so look out for the postman. Then you'll receive final confirmation of your flight times about two weeks before you fly, that's when things get really exciting. If there's anything at all that I can do to help in the meantime, remember my name is Chris, this is my card and there's my number. You guys are going to have a brilliant time.'

That's five star!

Actions

Three keys to a great script:

1 Write it down. Think about the words you like to use and the way they will flow.
2 Read it out loud five times. Make small adjustments each time until you like it. It will still feel false the first few times you use it but once it's committed to memory it will flow easily.
3 Be prepared to deviate slightly to say the right thing at the right time but generally stick to the basic script.

21

Telephone service

'It's a brilliant day at Michael Heppell. This is Ruth speaking, how may I help?'

That's how my staff answer the phone every time you call us. Cheerful and upbeat. It immediately lifts people. It sets the tone for the rest of the conversation. It gets us noticed. I love being in our office and hearing people answering the phone. I love ringing the office and hearing people answer the phone.

Then when we call other organisations ... you know what it's like. Often it's the company name blurted out, followed by a couldn't care less 'How may I help?'

'Only One Star, how may I help?'

But usually it's just the company name.

'Only One Star.'

Dull, dull, double dull and not very five star. So step one is to work out how you are going to answer the phone. It doesn't have to be 'It's a brilliant day ...' but why not choose a much better welcome than you are using right now?

Here are a few thoughts for our fake company called Only One Star.

'Welcome to Only One Star, this is Heather, how may I help?'

'Hello, this is Heather at Only One Star, how may I help?'

'Thank you for taking the time to call Only One Star, how can we help you today?'

If you called Only One Star, which way would you like the phone to be answered?

Now we've answered the phone, what's next?

Have you ever had a telephone conversation with someone and they just didn't sound interested in you? That's because they weren't. They may have said the right words in the right order but their body language and tone told a different story.

And you heard it.

Just because a person on the phone **can't be seen** it doesn't mean you can't **feel them**.

In fact, when talking to someone on the phone it's best to exaggerate your physiology (what you do with your body) and slightly exaggerate your tone. Here's how to do it:

1 Sit up or, even better, stand up.

2 Look slightly upwards.

3 Smile – smiles can be heard over the phone.

4 Stay focused – no matter what else is going on around you.

5 Create a visual image of the person you are talking to – make them look happy and nice.

6 Use the person's name.

7 At the end of the conversation remember to say a sincere thank you.

Do those seven simple steps on every call you make and you'll quickly see the difference in the quality of your conversations and how your customers respond to you.

But if you want to really excel, dive into 'Advanced telephone service' in the following chapter.

22

Advanced telephone service

We've got the basics of creating a five star telephone style, so what's next? Great five star telephone service practitioners have habits that others can only dream about. At first they seem a little complicated, but very quickly you'll get used to them.

Voice mirroring

You may have heard of 'matching and mirroring' as a way to build rapport. It's a great tool to use but most people limit it to face-to-face meetings. On the phone it works just as well.

There are three important actions to mirror on the phone:

1 Key words.

2 Personal phrases.

3 Visual, auditory or kinaesthetic cues.

Let's start with key words and personal phrases. As you are engaged in a conversation, make a note of any key words the person uses. You'll know them as they'll stand out of the conversation. When you talk to them your task is to replay at least three of the words or phrases.

Here's an example where a business traveller is looking for a room in a hotel.

'I'd like a nice big bed in a quiet part of the hotel, please. I'm not bothered about a view as I'll be working and having a bite to eat in my room. Do all of your rooms have plenty of sockets?'

Our traveller rang two hotels with the same request. Read the two responses and guess which one got the business.

'We have a queen-bedded room available in the west wing, our "Guestronomic" room service is available 24 hours and every room has full internet access and 240-volt power supplies.'

Or

'I've got a room here with a lovely big bed in the quietest part of our hotel. We'd be happy to serve you a bite to eat in your room and I can confirm all our rooms have plenty of sockets.'

As you can see, the first person gave all the correct information but it was right out of the brochure. Our traveller isn't bothered about a 'queen bed' or that the room service is called 'Guestronomic' or that the voltage is 240. The second person listened, noted and replayed several key words and personal phrases. Our traveller used the term 'lovely big bed' so got 'a lovely big bed'. And used the term 'bite to eat' so is going to get 'a bite to eat'. See how many more you can spot in those two simple sentences.

Not only is this very powerful, it's also great fun. Give it a test – you'll love it.

Here are some classic mismatches (both on and off the phone) – how we can get the subtle things wrong and what we could say:

Customer	Wrong Answer ✗	Right Answer ✔
I need it urgently	We'll send it quickly	We'll send it urgently
Can you fit me in?	We have a vacancy	We can fit you in
How much are the fees?	The cost is	The fees are
I'd like it in scarlet	We have it in red	We have it in scarlet
Does it contain dairy?	There's no milk in it	No, it doesn't contain dairy
Can I return this?	We can take it back	Yes, you can return it

Primary styles

The next area to look at is using and understanding people's primary styles. Most people fit under one of three primary styles:

Visual

Auditory

Kinaesthetic

When you're on the telephone to a visual person you will recognise that they tend to use visual 'cues'. For example, they will say things like 'I've seen your product and it looks very interesting, could you send me a brochure so I could look at it in more detail?'

When you're on the telephone to an auditory person you will recognise that they tend to use audio cues. For example, they will say things like, 'I've heard about your product and it sounds very interesting, could you tell me a bit more about it, I'd like to hear some more detail.'

When you're on the telephone to a kinaesthetic person you will recognise that they tend to use kinaesthetic cues. For example, 'I know about your product and it feels like something I could be interested in. Can you describe what it does and keep me in touch with future development plans?'

You will also notice that the three types of people tend to talk at different rates. Visual people tend to talk very quickly. You've heard the expression 'a picture is worth a thousand words': well, visual people try to fit in all one thousand words as they picture what they would like to say.

Auditory people tend to be more paced and often have a wider vocabulary.

Kinaesthetic people tend to be very slow and often they will pause as they try to get in touch with their feelings. At this point auditory and visual people tend to jump in and try to finish sentences for them. Kinaesthetic people really hate this so if you are talking to one, let them finish.

You can have a lot of fun by attempting to understand primary styles early in a conversation, then communicating back to the other person in that particular style for the rest of the conversation.

So why should we take time to learn and apply these ideas?

Basically **people like people** who are like **themselves**.

In simple terms, if we know what these primary styles are and use them, at a subconscious level the people we are talking to think that we are more like them. And if we like people who are like ourselves, we create a much better customer experience.

Like learning any new skill, the more you do it, the easier it gets and quite soon you'll be able to mirror a whole range of people's tones, styles and nuances.

Checklist of words and phrases to look out for:

Visual	Auditory	Kinaesthetic
See	Sounds	Feel
Look	Listen	Hard
Picture	Hear	Get a handle
Vision	Deaf	Touch
Reveal	Rings a bell	Grasp
Imagine	Silence	Concrete
Show	Deafening	Stroke
Clear	Tune in	Finger
Image	Hush	Gut

At the end of the day most people aren't totally visual, auditory or kinaesthetic; they tend to be a mixture of VAK (visual, auditory and kinaesthetic), but many do have a primary style which they use to communicate with, and this is the one to listen out for, feel and focus in on.

23

Voicemail, answering machines and automated call queue systems

ow many times have you called somebody and heard this kind of message:

'I'm either on the phone or away from my desk right now. Please leave a message and I'll get back to you as soon as I can. Please speak clearly after the tone.'

Are you really going to set the world alight with that one? Why not create a voicemail that promotes what you do in a five star way and at the same time does the important job of encouraging people to leave a message?

Imagine if you were a plumber and your voicemail said, 'I'm sorry I can't answer the phone personally right now as I'm out on a job installing some quality pipework for a valued customer. Leave me a message after the tone and I could do the same for you.'

What if you were a photographer who specialised in portraits and your voicemail said, 'Right now, I'm helping somebody capture a family image so they can treasure this moment for a lifetime. Please leave your message after the flash.'

What if you worked in an accounts department and the message said, 'I'm sorry I can't take your call right now as I'm taking a break from my desk to make sure that when I come back I'm fresh as a daisy and able to make the numbers match, the payments accurate and get the invoices out on time.'

I would love to call a company that has a queue system that starts off with, 'You've probably noticed it's one of those system things where you have to press a button just to get to the next menu. Well, we do this because when it works, it's much more efficient and honestly it does benefit you. So here we go, time to make your first choice, and press one ...'

Recently I've noticed that some people are leaving unique daily messages, especially on mobiles. That's a great idea because it makes that person seem very real. However, they then say something like, 'It's Monday the 21st, I'm in meetings most of today so please leave a message and I'll get back to you.'

Wouldn't it be brilliant if instead it said,

> 'It's Monday the 21st and today I have the privilege of meeting with some customers in the morning and after a quick lunch I'm going to a product launch to see the latest software designed to enhance our business. So don't hang up. Instead leave me a message and I'll get back to you either later on today or first thing tomorrow morning.'

I know it's not suitable for everybody reading this book to have a message like that, but I would bet that over half of those reading could.

Be careful though. Don't make your message so long and entertaining that by the time your personal message ends the caller has hung up. Be aware how often you get the same people leaving you a message – if you get the same people all the time they may just need a couple of words. I have a friend whose message says, 'Dan. Speak at beep.' Dan is a man of few words but cheap mobile bills.

Go on, I dare you to re-record your voicemail message right now, have some fun and take a risk.

Bonus Bit

Here are 21 great words to use in a message (not all of them!):

Promise	Missed	Quickly
Grateful	Understand	The best
You	Short	Personally
Changing	Making	Value
Please	Clearly	Brilliant
Thank you	Magic	Appreciate
Earliest	Rapid	Will

Wee Wow™

'Out of office' replies on emails are often written with about 10 seconds' thought and 30 seconds' typing time (I know it's because you are usually about to go on holiday – yippee!) but they should always have a part on *what to do* and *who to contact'* if it's urgent. You don't want your customers wasting their time or your organisation's time by having to call in or, worse still if they can't get you, could they call your competition?

Here's a transcript of a wonderful Out of Office message.

Oh no! I'm so sorry you've received this out of office message. It's true, I'm not here, but I'd like to make it up to you. My colleague Gavin is not only better looking than me, but he's dealing with things while I'm not here. I'm back on Wednesday (5th) but if it can't wait (and why should you?) then please contact Gavin on____ or email him at Gavin@_____ Please don't mention the good looking bit.

Thank you, Sam

24

It's not what you say

'It's serious. Your car needs a new differential. We are talking thousands, not hundreds, and we can't do the work for a few days.'

t wasn't what I wanted to hear . . . The service receptionist in the garage was just doing her job, but she could have learned so much from the technician (remember when they were called mechanics?) who had diagnosed the problem a few moments earlier. Here's what Paul Smith at Mercedes in Newcastle said: 'Mr Heppell, I've got some good news. We've caught the problem before it had a serious impact on your car. It's a new "diff" that's needed. It's not a big job to fit it, so we will see if we can get you booked in as soon as possible.'

'How much will it cost?'

'To be honest, it's not a cheap part but you have a really nice car and you look like a guy who wants things done right.'

So the technician told me the same message as the receptionist and added a few words that made me feel happy that my family and I were not in imminent danger. I felt reassured that it was the right thing to do and my car would soon be back on the road.

Fifteen minutes later the harbinger of doom gave me the same message and did all she could to make me feel low!

Why? My guess is that the receptionist has no idea of the impact she has on people when communicating in that way. She's 'just doing her job'. Or it could be that she likes the idea of a little bit of drama. Some people thrive on drama and negativity.

We've all heard the expression 'It ain't what you do it's the way that you do it.' This example is the same but this time it's 'It ain't what you say it's the way that you say it.'

I had a friend who was made redundant. When I asked how she felt, she said, 'I'm OK, but I'm worried for my boss, he couldn't have been nicer. It was really hard for him and he was so sympathetic. I'm lucky to have had him as my boss.'

I'm thinking, '**Wow**, what did he **say**?'

It turns out that the company had to make 20 people redundant to survive. Two managers each had to tell ten of their staff the news. My friend was let down by the nice guy. The other one had no idea how to give people bad news and ended up with four out of his ten considering unfair dismissal, bad mouthing him and the company, and trying to persuade the others to make a claim as well. Not one of the people who worked for my friend's boss wanted to take any further action.

What are you saying (and more importantly, how are you saying it) to your customers, colleagues, friends, family members? *Take time to focus on telling people news in a way that you would want to hear it.* It's not about lying, exaggeration or distortion. It's about giving people information in a positive way, in a way that you would find acceptable. In fact let's forget 'acceptable'; what about communicating in a brilliant way?

You will **feel awesome**. The people around you will **feel great** and, who knows, you may just get what you are looking for a **little bit faster**.

Wee Wow™

Open your hands outwards when telling people news that could be better. It's good body language, which symbolises genuine regret.

PART 4

Boiler room basics

You can smile, sing and dance all day, but if your basics aren't brilliant, your customers will quickly find someone else who has their own sparkling systems.

25

Embracing new technology

I have a problem.

When I first wrote 5 *Star Service* in 2006, a mention of Twitter would have been a miracle — it hadn't been invented.

In the last edition (published in 2010) I suggested that some 'early adopters' were embracing Twitter as a method of engaging with their customers. I gave an example of how one business communicated with its customers while they travelled on its trains. Yes, live at their seat, travelling at 125 mph.

Wow — and at the time that was leading edge.

Sitting at my desk today in March 2015, I'm stuck. I know I should be writing about how to use the latest technology to engage your customers, understand their needs, then wow them via binary brilliance.

The challenge is, by the time this book is published it will already be out of date.

That's not the same for the other chapters. The vast majority of the ideas I share in those are timeless.

So I've sat for a long time asking: Why?

If you're interested, here's my thought process, using the power of 'Why?'

Why does the *Embracing new technology* chapter date so quickly?

Because technology changes so fast.

Why?

Because the demand for the latest and best is so high.

Why?

Because we are dissatisfied with what we have.

Why?

Because we always want more.

Bingo. It's not about the technology; it's about the customer's demand — the need for more.

The chances of any customers demanding less in the foreseeable future is highly unlikely. So I'm faced with a dilemma. Do I write about how to use the latest technology to improve your service, or do I dig deeper?

Let's dig.

For a business, just opening a company Facebook page, signing up to Twitter or belonging to any social network is pointless without the right 'intent'.

New technology doesn't provide better levels of service. It's just a useful tool. An enabler.

Here's a little something to think about. Live Chat is being hailed as one of the greatest developments in customer service since the Suggestion Box.

I went into deep experiential research mode and started testing 'live chat'. I spent 2 days exploring the world of the virtual live chat assistant and guess what I discovered? Apple are brilliant at it and most of the banks are rubbish.

That has nothing to do with Live Chat and everything to do with people.

It's the same with Twitter. Twitter is the perfect platform for organisations to get real-time feedback from their customers. BUT, and this is a massive but, the people tweeting on behalf of your business have got to be brilliant.

Here's the major difference between a call-centre and online responses. Your online conversation is normally public and will be there forever.

So you'd better be brilliant.

I talked to Nick Wood who is the Social Media Manager for Virgin East Coast Trains. I wanted to chat to Nick because over the last few years I've followed their Twitter feed and interacted with them on many occasions.

Often it's good news. I use my @MichaelHeppell Twitter account to compliment a crew, say how much I'm enjoying the service and share ideas.

Other times it's to have a rant. Like sharing a frustration, or to point out (with a photograph) that our train is actually on fire, so stop saying it's just an 'engine failure'.

Nick describes social media as a 'Giant goldfish bowl', adding, 'Everyone can see you and everyone has an opinion'.

He encourages his team to use their intuition and if it feels right to communicate in a certain way, then do it.

Nick believes the most important part of his team's role is to reassure, to let travellers know that the Social Media Team are travelling companions. But, most importantly, they care and they are on the side of the customer. See for yourself @Virgin_ TrainsEC

Now let's ramp this up a notch.

The next wave of technology doesn't involve people at all. IVA (Intelligent Virtual Assistant) technology could be a brilliant idea. You don't even have to pay someone to answer your customer's queries.

But, and this is another big but, if you use this type of technology, there's a golden rule. Manage your customer's expectations. Tell your customer right from the start they are talking to a computer not a person. There are already some organisations who are close to telling out and out lies about who you're communicating with, and they are going to get busted.

The most valuable online technology comes when it's linked with real people.

Your order will be delivered between 9 and 12 today = so what.

Your order will be delivered between 10.34 and 11.34 today by our driver, Liam. Click here to follow his route = magic.

And when Liam delivers the parcel, I already know his name. We have a bit of banter; he tells me he's 15 mins ahead of schedule and suddenly we're mates.

Tweet this: New technology means nothing without brilliant people behind it. #5StarService by @MichaelHeppell.

26

RADAR
thinking™

What do you do if you have a **common problem** that comes up time after time?

You know the customer isn't going to be happy but you can't do anything about it. It really is outside your control.

Radar equipment on planes makes a pilot aware of any obstructions to their planned flight path. So a mountain range would be visible on a radar system and a new flight path would be calculated. No one expects a mountain to move.

Radar is a brilliant invention; it detects problems and makes us aware of them.

RADAR thinking™ takes situations where you previously thought you had a nightmare and turns them into customer service dreams.

Use RADAR as an acronym:

Realise

Assess

Decide

Act

Review

Realise – that you actually have a problem. Get your head out of the sand and take a look at the regular challenges your customers face. Is it delivery times? Sub-contractors? Costs? Customer stupidity?

Once you have a list ...

Assess – have a really good brainstorm and throw lots of ideas into the pot. If you really are going to have a powerful brainstorm, make sure you use the three golden rules:

1   Write every idea down.

2   Keep it positive (ban anyone who says we've tried that before and it didn't work).

3   Allow everyone an opportunity to participate.

Once you have assessed all your ideas …

Decide – which ideas you are going to use and which ones you are going to park (or bin) for another day. Take the very best ideas and make sure they complement the real problem (go back to 'Realise' and check).

Once you have one or two that you are committed to …

Act – decisions without actions are pretty worthless. Have you heard the story of the four frogs sitting on the log? One decided to jump off. How many frogs were left? The answer is four because the frog only *decided* to jump off, he didn't actually do it! Ensure you put your ideas into practice swiftly and ensure that everyone knows what you are doing.

Once you have the ideas in place …

Review – take time to fine-tune or, if needs be, ditch an idea. Forget about that nonsense of 'get it right the first time' – go for getting it right by doing it. There aren't many ideas that changed the world by needing to be right the first time. Author's note: if you are a pilot reading this, the 'get it right the first time' idea *does* apply to you!

Once understood, you can use the RADAR technique as part of your weekly meetings or monthly staff training. The more people who are involved with the ownership of the ideas, the better they work.

Next, I'm going to give you three examples of RADAR thinking™ at its best.

27

RADAR thinking™ at work

Here are three examples of RADAR thinking™ being used to turn a regular challenge into a wonderful customer service experience.

1   I guess no customer service book would be complete without an example from Disney. Epcot in Orlando, Florida, is Disney's biggest park and as you would expect has a very big car park. If you have ever been (and driven there) you'll know the scale is huge – the Epcot car park alone can take up to 20,000 cars.

Logistically to get everyone from their cars to the park at the start of the day or from the park to their cars at the end of the day is a huge task so it doesn't help when a weary family gets to the end of a long day and tells a Disney cast member (their name for staff) that they can't remember where they've parked their car. This would be a nuisance if it happened to a dozen or so families but on busy days up to 500 people could have lost their cars.

Conventional thinking would be to suggest to the customer how utterly thick they have been and suggest they wait until everyone else has gone home. Then one of the remaining cars in the 30-acre car park would be theirs – and you hope they've learned a valuable lesson.

It was suggested at one point that Disney could have a lost car waiting area where families could shelter, watch cartoons and purchase snacks. Then when the car park cleared, a special 'Find your car' train would leave with everyone frantically pressing their remote key fobs until some lights flashed. Good fun and a nice idea but at the end of a long day what do you want? That's right – you just want your car back.

Here's how they fixed the problem, allowing over 90 per cent of people to find their car in less than five minutes.

When you are collected from the car park, a road train takes you from your row in the car park to the entrance. The train driver asks you to remember the name of your car park (all named after Disney characters) and the row you have parked in. He even gets you to say it out loud. But most people are so excited (and exhausted) by the end of the day that a car park name and row number are just a distant memory.

So (and here's the Disney magic) the driver who picks you up also writes the exact time he or she arrived, the name of the car park and the row number. Then should you lose your car the cast member assigned to help you locate it will ask, 'Do you remember what time you arrived?' In most cases people remember the time they arrived because they are: (a) proud of the fact they got there early, (b) rushing because the gates have opened or are about to open, (c) thinking about how much of their day has been lost because they are arriving late (Disney tickets aren't cheap!). Then they look down the list for your arrival time and reveal that you were parked in 'Pluto 15' and a wave of familiarity washes over you.

This simple yet effective system **thrills customers**, frees up **valuable** staff **time** and can be **duplicated effortlessly**.

2 Olympian Furniture in Edinburgh and Glasgow is an amazing company. Not only does it provide great furniture but also the staff look after you like you are the only person in the world. It's a pleasure to shop there and they love to have you even if you don't buy anything. However, they have a problem.

Most of the furniture is hand-made and can take up to 12 weeks from order to delivery. Excited customers would fall in love with a beautiful piece of furniture and proudly place an order. They would be told, 'It may take up to 12 weeks for delivery'. As you can imagine, once ordered, when do they want it? That's right – *now* or sooner if possible. The brilliant staff at Olympian used to say, 'It will be worth the wait.' Very true, but customers would still be thinking, 'I want it now.'

So after learning about RADAR they realised that the problem wasn't going to go away unless they started to stock pre-packed lower-quality goods and that was never going to happen.

They **realised** they had a problem with the waiting time.

They **assessed** what they could do and involved every member of the company, including delivery and back-office staff.

They **decided** to turn this wait into a feature by actually building it into their sales presentation.

They took **action** and wrote an overview for all staff to share with customers explaining that to have a piece of furniture of this quality takes longer. They would explain what would happen after their order was placed, how the leather is dyed in Italy or how the wood is polished using a special process that can't be hurried. They would explain that the furniture is delivered complete and must be robust enough for travel and how the delivery team will bring the furniture to them only when it has had a final inspection.

While **reviewing** the strategy, they have continued to improve on this technique, showing customers why it's more than 'worth the wait' and it's part of the quality of the Olympian experience.

3   My friend Nicola called me and said, 'Dyson vacuum cleaners use RADAR.' I've never worked with them so I'm sure they don't call their thinking RADAR, but their idea was simple and classy.

Nicola's Dyson stopped working. After three years of trouble-free vacuuming it just stopped. The first bit of RADAR thinking™ was obvious when she found the helpline number on the cleaner (because we don't keep manuals). Second was when she called on a Saturday night there was someone there because 'people use Dysons at all times, so we have to be here at all times', advised the customer service agent. A quick diagnostic predicted a burnt-out motor. An engineer would be sent out and it would be a maximum of £50 no matter what the problem was.

The engineer arrived, on time, looking smart, and sure enough the problem was the motor, which he replaced. And he changed the cable because that looked a little worn. And fitted a new plug because the other one was cracked. And replaced the filter and gave the whole machine a smarten up (all for the agreed £50).

Then RADAR really kicked in as the engineer asked Nicola whether she knew how to wash the filter or that she was supposed to do it every six months. No and no came the reply. It turns out that the number one reason why a motor burns out is because users don't clean the filter and you really should do it every six months. So he showed Nicola how to take it out, how to wash it and how to replace it.

Then he asked whether she had a PC and took her to the Dyson website and registered her to receive a six-monthly email reminder to clean the filter, because we could be better at remembering stuff like that.

One other thing, while she was on the site she was offered 10 per cent off attachments and ended up buying another £60 worth of products!

28

Designing fantastic service

I'**ve met Sir Jonathan Ive.** Sorry about the name drop and I appreciate that may (or may not) impress you. But if you've ever held an iPad, iPhone, iPod or an iAnything, it's Sir Johnny Ive and his team who made you go all gooey, become unrealistically attached to an inanimate object and think 'want, want, want, must have'.

Apple design the very best technology products. And that doesn't happen by accident. Teams of people spend thousands of hours making your iThing simple to use and stunning to look at.

You know that the most unassuming designs often take masses of hard work to make them appear simple. You know your customers crave simple, and yet very few people take the time to design simple, superb service.

Working with hundreds of organisations, I've seen various levels of commitment to designing innovative five star service. So many companies get very excited at the start of a process with their 'off-site' meetings and brainstorming sessions. Then they wheel in the 'we're so well known we only use abbreviations' external consultants who happily charge mega bucks to ask (with an ever so serious face), 'Well, you tell me, what do you think ... '

That's an expensive route. It's fine if you want to spend a small fortune, but how do you do that on a one star budget?

The fashion designer Wayne Hemmingway once gave me some advice. Not fashion advice — it's too late for that! Some years ago my daughter had her heart set on being a designer, so I asked Wayne whether he had any advice for her.

'Does she make her own clothes?' was his first question. Was she just into the image and the glamour, or was she prepared for hard work, and had she already started to create something beyond a sketch? His next piece of advice was that she should make me a shirt and other clothes she could sell to her friends. All this at 13 years of age? He was right.

Our discussion led me to a conclusion. If you really want to get into a prestigious fashion school and you've been making and selling clothes for five years, you're going to have a pretty big tick on your Supporting Statement.

'The secret isn't in the knowing, it's in the doing.' That's something I say a lot. It's the same with **designing brilliant service.**

Think about it. You can have all the theory in the world, but, until you actually test something, you have no idea whether it's going to work or not.

In the late 1930s the first 'crash tests' in the motor industry were carried out with a view to making car travel safer. This was almost 70 years after the first recorded motor vehicle accident victim. Mary Ward was killed by her cousin's experimental steam-powered motor vehicle. Interestingly, Mary Ward's great granddaughter is the actress Lalla Ward, who was once married to Time Lord Tom Baker but is now espoused to ethologist and evolutionary biologist Richard Dawkins. I digress in a Bill Brysonesque manner, so back to the point.

Once the researchers realised that death needn't be an inconvenient by-product of car travel, they couldn't get enough of testing. Initially they used dead bodies, followed by animals and volunteers before some bright spark invented the crash test dummy.

Modern crash test dummies measure everything, so clever designers can use that information to create safer, happier motoring.

So how do you design world-class service? Here are seven keys and a simple process to get you started.

1   Know what you want. If you don't have clear objectives, how will you know you've achieved what you set out to achieve?

2   Get other people involved. Do your own version of a Public Consultation and listen carefully to what everybody has to say. You don't have to take all the advice on board, and remember; people will soon stop sharing if you constantly interrupt.

3   Create two piles of cards: 'all the things that can go wrong' and 'all the things that must go right'.

4 Share the cards around your team and allow everyone an opportunity to build on the 'rights' and eliminate the 'wrongs'.

5 Lay out the cards showing the 'flow' of service. This should show the links, the strong points, the potential weaknesses, etc.

6 Run the sequence forwards *and* backwards asking these three questions:

i How is the customer feeling?

ii How are we feeling?

iii What can we change or do better?

7 Once you have your 'service route' planned out, ensure individuals have responsibility for particular areas (and where more work is necessary) and the timescales for making it happen. Then review the system on a regular basis.

By making your **thinking three-dimensional** and running the sequences forwards and backwards you will **locate** many of the **potential challenges**.

Bonus Bit

When you run your service sequence, have some gold stars. Give a star to each part of the sequence that would outshine your customer's expectations. The goal is to get a minimum of five stars in every sequence.

29

Spanners and Heroes

ere's a great game you can play as a team to learn about and improve your customer service. You'll need:

- a pile of A6 cards
- pens
- some coloured wool
- some pictures of spanners and superheroes.

I love the expression 'spanner in the works'. It conjures up a very visual representation of how customer service can go so wrong: a wonderful complex piece of machinery is whirring away beautifully and then someone drops in a big ugly spanner, the machine coughs and splutters, shards of metal start to fly all around, steam and smoke burst forth and then the whole thing grinds to a halt.

I also love the expression 'You're a hero'. It's often said when someone saves the day and does something out of the ordinary to make sure everyone is happy.

Here's how you play the game.

- **Step One** Decide on a customer service issue. For this example we are going to imagine you work for a company that sells tickets with hospitality for sporting events and you are selling packages for the Wimbledon semi-final.

- **Step Two** Plan the customer service experience and as a team write down every step on an A6 card. You can go into as much detail as you like with this. So in our example something like:

1 Bulk-buy 40 tickets for a sporting event.
2 Place an advert in the sports pages of a newspaper.
3 Organise somebody to take the calls and alert them that an advert has been placed in Y paper for Z day.
4 Take incoming calls.
5 Explain the package to a potential customer.
6 Customer buys the tickets.
7 Credit card transaction takes place.
8 Tickets posted to the customer.

That's a very simple way to look at the process. You may wish to go into a lot more detail. Once all the cards are completed and all the links are made by attaching wool. Now the fun can really begin.

Split into two teams and have (depending on numbers) one or two referees. Toss a coin to decide which team will be the Spanners and which team will be the Heroes. Each member of the Spanner team gets one spanner card and each member of the Hero team gets two hero cards.

The Spanners then need to decide where they are going to place 'a spanner in the works'. The idea is to create a situation that has the maximum negative effect from the customer's perspective. Then they play a spanner card and place it on the part of the process they want to affect and explain what their spanner means. The referee decides whether it is a fair and realistic problem to have.

So in our example we may decide that a spanner in the works would be not to alert those appointed to receive the calls about the advert and the day it is due to appear. The Spanners explain that this would cause confusion because people would be calling in larger numbers than normal, they wouldn't know what advert the customer was responding to and huge amounts of stress and negativity would be caused which in turn would be passed on to the customer. A real result for the Spanners.

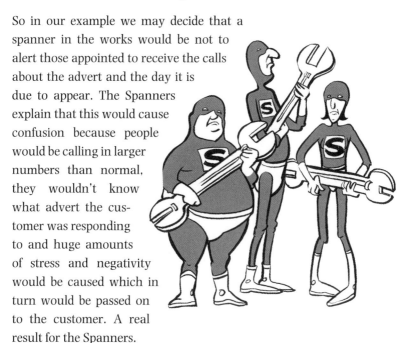

The Heroes then have to decide what they are going to do with their two cards.

The first fixes the problem, the second enhances the system.

So they may choose to use their first card to fix the problem by focusing on a flexible attitude with the staff and by having several staff multi-skilled so they can take over the phones should they be caught out during unexpected busy periods. The second card has to enhance a part of the current system. They may choose to enhance the piece they are working on, making it bulletproof so it doesn't happen again. Or they may choose to enhance another area such as putting in two customer service calls, one to ensure they have the tickets soon after the expected arrival date and one the day after the event to see how it went and to tell them about other events they may be interested in.

Once each team has played their cards, decide which items are going to be made a real part of your organisation's ways of working.

Remember – the aim of the game is for the **Heroes to win**!

Wee Wow™

People tend to play games the same way they play life. A good facilitator will observe how people react and use this to create discussion at the end of each live issue.

30

Suppliers are customers too

It's all about price. Isn't it? Well yes and no. We all want a good price but I've yet to meet anyone who would admit to wanting to sacrifice great service for a little extra discount. But the fact is people do. And they do it with their suppliers financially, emotionally and habitually.

Remember this.

Customers can be defined as anyone you have an interaction with.

This means your suppliers are your customers too and how you treat them will have a major impact on your other customers – the ones who pay your bills.

After many years in business I'm happy to say that I believe we have found a group of brilliant suppliers who are committed to great service. I don't know how good they are for their other clients but I do know they are brilliant for us. I know that because I've worked hard to help them be brilliant suppliers. Here are a few of the things we've done in the past and do now.

Invited them to participate in our events.

Thanked them in writing and let individuals' bosses know how much we appreciate their great service.

Referred them to other companies.

Invited them to our Christmas party.

Sent them copies of my books.

Written about them in newsletters.

Created links to their businesses on my website.

Taken them out for lunch to talk about challenges.

Shared with them future plans and listened to their advice.

Paid our bills on time.

Getting the best out of your suppliers is exactly the same as getting the very best out of your most loyal staff, and if you want to create a brilliant five star experience then having brilliant five star suppliers is a must.

I really struggle with organisations who bring in companies or new staff whose sole aim is to reduce costs. What if you employed a member of staff whose sole role was to improve the relationships, loyalty and service from your suppliers? Do you think you might find some cost savings in there too?

And does it work? I really do believe so. I know that if we have an IT problem, Norman or Neil from KF Datawright will dive into action and go the extra mile to get it fixed, often working overtime or on problems at home. And it's not just the little businesses that can do this. We have a fantastic relationship with HSBC and I'll continue to write for Pearson, not because they are the biggest publishers in the world but because they have built a relationship with me that enables me to get my message to my customers.

Here's a simple way to check, and then improve, your relationships with your suppliers.

1   Create a list – here's a clue, they are probably sending you invoices so just print off your creditors.

2   Consider what you want from each supplier, ask your colleagues, then write it down.

3   Let them know. Meet up, pick up the phone, have a suppliers event.

4   Keep them informed. Especially when they get it right. Thank-you cards, personal cards, small gifts, etc. have a massive impact.

5   Pay your bills on time and, if you can't, communicate why you can't and when you will.

6   If you get a better offer from another supplier, talk to your existing one before switching. There may be a very good reason why they charge a little more. Who knows, they may even price match.

31

Making the mundane marvellous

Which part of your customer interaction could be described as mundane? Completing forms, being left on hold, queuing? Even the most exciting businesses have moments that their customers find mundane. Let's start with a classic – queuing!

No one enjoys queuing; it's lost time and you can guarantee it creates stress. Here are my top five most stressful queues. See whether you agree.

1 Having your call put on hold and not knowing how long you'll have to wait

2 Supermarket checkouts

3 The 'carriage queue' on the station platform – especially if you don't have a reserved seat

4 Airport check-in for the homeward flight.

5 The taxi rank at Kings Cross station.

What can you do to make your customers' queuing experience more enjoyable?

1 Acknowledge the queue. If it's busy let people know. Give them a realistic expectation of what will be happening.

2 Give them something to do. Theme parks are the masters of this, often making the last 30 minutes' wait part of the experience.

3 Throw more resources at it. Is it beneath the MD to pick up a phone and take a customer service call?

4 Entertain. 'On hold' recordings are at best dull. How about a couple of jokes or some useful information?

5 And how about a sincere apology or acknowledgement that we've had to wait?

However, there's more to the mundane than just queuing. Filling in forms, refuelling your car, waiting rooms, watching a screen while your emails download, they're all a bit mundane and a bit boring. But what if you were to change that?

And it doesn't need to be a big budget flat-screen TV or special effects phenomena. Here's a simple one to get you started.

I was refuelling my car the other day when I looked up and saw the attendant staring at me. I gave a smile and little wave and she just continued to stare back blankly.

I turned to see whether there was anything more interesting happening over my shoulder, there wasn't. Now what could she have done?

Waved back and offered a cheery smile? Yup, that would be great three star service. Or what if she had waved at me first, or given a little thumbs-up, or simply acknowledged her customer? Let's make that four star. And for five star…? Well what would you do?

Here are a few more ideas to make the mundane marvellous. Some may be a perfect fit for you. Some may need a tweak. Some will be completely left-field but I'm sure they'll get you thinking.

Play music at bus stops.

Have a lucky car draw in a car park queue.

Have up-to-date, interesting, clean reading material in your reception.

Give your customer a chance to win their software free during a download.

Use a comedian (politically correct of course) for your 'on hold' recording.

Add a few encouraging comments on boring forms, 'Almost there', 'Last page', 'You did it!'.

Give staff training in non-verbal communication. Then use it!

Have a free Monday draw on a commuter train for season ticket holders.

Test, test, test is the trick.

No one enjoys a long wait. Queuing has become the butt of many jokes; 'We apologise that all lines are busy, please hold . . . ' drives you mad.

All customers have an 'internal' clock which starts ticking as soon as they join a queue, order a meal, are put on hold. Once this clock starts ticking it's only a matter of time before the internal alarm goes off.

Ritz Carlton and Apple use creative ways to *reset* the internal clocks of their customers.

If a waiter notices you've been waiting too long in a Ritz Carlton restaurant they are empowered to pop into the kitchen and bring you a complimentary amuse-bouche. As soon as this tasty snack arrives, your eyes open, you smile, feel valued and your internal clock is reset. The starters can wait another five minutes.

In an Apple Store, if your appointment is delayed at the Genius Bar, the staff will suggest you try out a new piece of technology while you wait. Even offering to come and find you when it's your turn.

All Apple equipment is turned on, connected to the internet and ready to use, your internal clock is reset and you are less likely to mind having to wait an additional few minutes for your appointment.

Who knows whether your idea will work unless you give it a go and learn from your successes and mistakes? Every time you test an idea you'll be raising your game and doing your bit towards making the mundane marvellous.

32

Systemise routines – personalise exceptions

How long does it take to make a Mojito? The bar crew at the Blue Marlin Beach Club in Ibiza make them in less than 30 seconds – further up the beach it takes four minutes. At €14 each, which bar would you like to own?

I spent a very pleasant afternoon one August researching this chapter, observing how the bar crews worked, coped with exceptions, wowed their customers and made a tidy profit too.

Now flip it and think about it from the customer's point of view. August in Ibiza is a busy time, bars like the Blue Marlin Beach Club can attract well over 1,000 people. That's a lot of hungry, thirsty people who want to get their drinks and head back to the sun.

The staff know their most popular drink is a Mojito and they have a pretty good idea of how many they will sell. So well before the first customer arrives, they have a pre-opening Mojito preparation session. They make up hundreds of glasses with lime, brown sugar and mint. They know how long it will stay fresh and they time it perfectly. Next they have designed and set up the bar so everything is to hand. Finally everything else is

stocked at one or two levels higher than requirement. They'll never run out of rum because the bar assistant replaces bottles when there are still four or five left. Ice is bought in precrushed and stored in an easy to reach central location. Each member of the bar team has their own utensils so there's no waiting around for a colleague to finish before they can make up your order. And finally (and most importantly) they look like they are having a ball!

Each part of the preparation and planning saves a chunk of time from a few seconds to a minute. And each saving of time is passed on to the customer.

Compare this with the beach bar just up the road. They start everything from scratch – which would be lovely if it was just you at the bar, chatting to the bartender as the sun sets. But there's not just you. It's five deep, everyone wants to be served and when you hear the person in front say, 'Four Mojitos please', there's an audible groan. They run out of rum, have to wait until their buddy has finished with the one 'muddler' and look completely exasperated.

The Blue Marlin has automated a routine and done it in such a way that the customer is delighted. Everyone likes to save time, even people chilling in Ibiza. The obvious question is, what can you do to automate your systems to make life easier for your customer?

Does your website have frequently asked questions?

Do you talk to each other about the most common challenges that crop up?

Do you observe how your competitors are running their systems and use the best of what they do and avoid the worst?

Could you shave a few seconds or minutes off your customer's wait time?

All of these ideas are simple, but not easy. They need time, effort and resources assigned to them. Then once you find your super system you can't relax – in fact you have to be prepared to deviate from it because it won't always be right and it won't always work.

The **last thing** a customer wants to hear is **why you can't** do something for them because you have '**a system**'.

Let's go back to the Blue Marlin and ask what they do when they get thrown an exception. Well, in the spirit of my five star study I ordered another couple of Mojitos (it's hard work doing all this research). This time I asked for one of them to have only a tiny amount of sugar but lots of mint. No problem for the crew who called it 'a special'. It took them just over a minute, no problem there but here's the best bit, when handing over the drinks the barman popped a different straw in to our high-mint low-sugar cocktail and with a smile said, 'That's your special one.'

Customers love routines to be speeded up, simplified and made more convenient, but never use this as a reason not to look out for the exception.

I hope the Blue Marlin continues to improve its Mojito-making system as I feel another research trip coming on!

33

The distraction of dirt

Clean = Good

Spotless = Five Star

'm writing this chapter on a train. It's big, seats hundreds of people and can travel at well over 100 miles an hour. I'm sitting in first class, which is a privilege I never take for granted, and your eyes (like mine) would water if you knew the cost of the tickets. There is a challenge though. It's a bit dirty. There are crumbs on the table from the last traveller, an unidentifiable stain on the window and the guard – sorry, revenue protection officer – has dirty nails. The latter was pointed out by Christine, who spots nasty nail fungi at 50 paces.

It's not nice is it? I have a friend who got off a plane because his seat table was filthy. His thinking was, 'If that's how they treat the tables, how well do they look after the engines?'

And it gets worse. My friend Tom decided he didn't want to buy a £50,000 car because the salesman had dirty shoes.

There's a famous story that Michael Eisner, the then chief executive officer of the Walt Disney Corporation, was showing a group of international executives around the Magic Kingdom. He walked across the street, picked up a piece of litter and threw it in the nearest bin. When one of the group suggested he must have staff to do that he replied, 'The cleanliness of Disney is everyone's responsibility.'

I've heard the story so many times that there's a little piece of me thinks they must plant the litter for every tour so he can make that point! And the point is obvious – isn't it? Or is it?

The level of **cleanliness** around your product or service **has to be immaculate**.

Not good, not left to the next person, not 'it will get better tomorrow'. I'm talking about immaculate now.

And I'm talking about you as well as your environment. You only get one chance to make a first impression and customers make judgements with their eyes long before they have experienced the service.

Here's a list of eight things you must consider.

1   Take a good hard look in the mirror. Honestly, how do you look? And what could be better?

2   Check your immediate environment. How is the entrance to your building? I know it's 'not your job' to keep it clean but it's not Michael Eisner's either.

3   Nasty one. How are the toilets? If you don't think they are peachy then what do you think your customers will think of them?

4   Surfaces, signs and stationery. If they are dirty, your customers will subconsciously associate that with your offering.

5   Smells. If NCP car parks can do a brilliant job eliminating and replacing some of the challenging smells their venues are faced with (and I don't think I need to explain any more here) then what can you do with your environment?

6   Tidy. Make it easy for people to be neat by giving or getting the right storage and encouraging a bit of basic Feng Shui thinking.

7   Hands. Bitten or dirty nails, picked skin and nicotine stains all add up to a poor personal service.

8   Body smell. Bad breath, BO and festering feet. If you *think* you have a bit of a body odour issue then the chances are you have! If you're worried that you may have bad breath you will be the last person to spot it! And if you think your feet smell a little, it's more than likely they're lifting! You need an honest Joe who'll tell you (and you can tell them) if there's a nasal nuisance to sort out.

34

Secret shopper

I **f you can afford it** (and maybe even if you can't), I would recommend you consider using a mystery shopping service to help you raise your game. Good ones help you to:

remove yourself from the process

identify what's wrong

recognise what's right

test your systems

improve your sales

help create or carry out training with your staff.

The basic idea is very simple. You brief a mystery shopping company with what you would like to find out. They shop, eat, call, etc. your organisation then give you feedback against the criteria you discussed in the initial briefing. There, it's that simple.

You need to have a very clear idea of what you want from a mystery shopper experience and you have to find someone who's on your wavelength.

The Secret Service (no not that one) is a mystery shopping company that specialises in making the whole experience enjoyable, educational and profitable. Its founder Linda Eastwood explained to me that, by getting the right mystery shopper company to help your business, you should increase your sales, improve staff loyalty and find out as much about what you're doing right as what you're doing wrong.

When I met with her she was keen to dismiss a few myths about mystery shopping. Here's a selection.

Myth One Don't tell your staff you are using a secret shopping company: that way you'll get feedback warts and all.

Do tell your staff! Why shouldn't they know that you're using secret shoppers? Don't you trust them? Because once they find out you're 'sending in the spies' they won't trust you.

Myth Two If you let your staff know won't they start to improve their level of service before your mystery shopper arrives, and won't that defeat the object?

Now your customer service is improving already – get it?

Myth Three It's good to use a mystery shopping company because if someone else catches them doing something wrong, then I'm not responsible.

But this is about everyone's responsibility. It may be that you have to face some home truths about your levels of training, systems and investment in your people. Are you ready for that?

Myth Four Won't it demoralise my staff?

That very much depends on how you treat the experience. Do it in a sneaky underhand way that focuses on what's wrong and yes you may demoralise them. Make it a fun experience that rewards what's right and staff will hope that they are being mystery shopped.

Myth Five We only have a small business, so I'll just ask my friends or family to help.

Often people with small businesses make the huge mistake of asking friends and family to mystery shop for them. Our friends then think they are doing us a huge favour by criticising everything from the colour of the wallpaper to the number of rings before someone picked up the phone. The result is a disillusioned owner with friends who have the impression that you have a rubbish business.

If you can't use a professional company, then how about using a member of a trade group you belong to? You could return the favour for them but remember to keep it positive.

Secret shopping is as much about observing people **doing things right** as it is about catching them doing things wrong.

PART 5

Navigating the negatives

You will get it wrong, drop the ball and cause some customers distress. Instead of worrying how you got into the crocodile's mouth, here's how to get out of it.

35

Complaints –
a chance to
shine!

Complaints are brilliant. This chapter gives five great reasons why complaints should be loved not loathed.

You should **love complaints** as they provide an opportunity to **save the day**, **learn from mistakes** and **become better**… but only if you know how.

Reason 1 – Now you know

Ignorance isn't bliss when it comes to customer dissatisfaction. Ignoring an issue doesn't make it go away – it makes it fester and grow, until eventually you feel out of control.

Knowing about a service issue is the first stage to fixing it. Yes it makes you feel slightly sick, especially if you're responsible. Yes you'll wish you hadn't heard it – especially if you care about your customer. And yes you'll be embarrassed – although perhaps you should be. But not for long. Being embarrassed doesn't change things. That's why there's reason number two.

Reason 2 – You get a chance to fix it

Even the best five star service advocates sometimes need a reason to kick some butt to get their point across. Being able to say to colleagues, 'We've had a complaint about this, who'd like to fix it?' makes an issue very immediate. After all, you don't want to receive a second complaint for the same problem do you?

Creating momentum and a desire to fix a problem when you receive a complaint is a good thing. It encourages you (and your team) to take action and overcome procrastination.

The next stage is to close the loop and let your customer know what you have done. Customers love it when you call them, thank them for their complaint, show you care and then explain what actions you have taken to fix it.

Reason 3 – Wake-up call

Now and then we all need a wake-up call. Yes you may be dealing with a 'professional complainer' – you know the type who just complains in an attempt to get free stuff. But if you share my belief that 99 per cent of people are good (see Chapter 8) then you have to take the professional complainer's complaint as seriously as you would any other.

And who knows ... they may be on to something. Imagine having a service culture that works so well that even the professional complainer has nothing to do but enjoy the process?

However, a wake-up call may be just what you need to encourage you to get your finger out and take some proactive service action.

Reason 4 – You learn

Or should I say, I *hope* you learn. Complaints take organisations through a steep learning curve. Then times change, new staff start, ways of working differ and, before you know it, the same problems reoccur.

Here's where a 'Complaints and Solutions Book' is handy. *This is not the same as a public complaints book.* Public complaints books are a crazy idea. Why would you create an environment that announces to customers (and staff), 'We are expecting your complaints'? No, this book is kept in your back office and is used to share with colleagues what happened, how the problem occurred, how you fixed it and, most importantly, what to do so it won't happen again.

Reason 5 – It's better they tell you

. . . than tell their friends. Most people don't complain when something has gone wrong. At least they don't complain to you. Instead they complain to their friends, neighbours, family, in fact anyone with ears. If you're lucky, you hear about the complaint second hand and wish they'd said something to you – but they don't so you didn't and they keep on telling their 'poor me' story.

So the next time you're listening to a complaint, it will make the process so much easier when in the back of your mind you're thinking, 'Well at least I know, and I can fix it,' or 'That certainly woke me up, and I can learn from it! And thank goodness they're telling me and not my other customers!'

A final thought. A complaint may sting for moment, but you'll get over it. A negative online complaint or review is there forever.

36

The blind spot

Every restaurant has one, every shop has one, every plane, every website, every customer experience. It's the place where customers, their issues and requirements simply aren't seen.

One of my favourite restaurants is Caffe Vivo in Newcastle. It's close to home, the food is amazing and the service is magic. We've been many times with family, friends and on business. We have never been disappointed.

Then one day a funny thing happened. We sat down for a meal and browsed the menu. With our mouths watering we were ready to order. And we waited ... and waited ... and, because I'm not very good at waiting, I did a slightly embarrassing wave before our order was taken.

The starters were sublime, the mains magnificent but when we were ready for more drinks the problem recurred. And I ended up waving.

The challenge became obvious – we were in the 'blind spot'. A part of the restaurant where the diners were less visible. Because we know how brilliant they are at Vivo it didn't affect our night – they have made enough

deposits in our emotional bank account to make a small withdrawal. However, the real issue was they didn't know they had an issue until we pointed it out.

That's the problem with the blind spot – it's not that you don't want to fix it, it's that you don't know it's there to fix. And blind spots come up everywhere. It could be:

the navigation of your website

the wording of a question on your application form

the layout of a shelf

a misleading pricing policy

a glitch in your software

being unaware of the attitude of someone on your teams.

So how do you identify your blind spot and, when you find it, what do you do?

Here's where your customers would love to help, but only if you ask them properly. If you say, 'How was everything today?' You'll get 'fine' as the response. Even when it wasn't.

So how about asking a better question after the 'fine' response? Something like, 'Thank you, but if there was one thing we could do better what would it be?'

You can find out more about this in Chapter 19 'Beware the silent customer'.

Another way to **find your blind spot** is to test, test, test; watch, watch, watch; act and review.

Most people do a little bit of testing, a tiny amount of watching and little or no acting or reviewing. You're not most people.

Computer game designers employ testers who play their games for hours at a time, running outrageous scenarios and monitoring the results.

If you were to really test your system, would it hold up? Test doing things at different times, test where your staff are positioned, test speeds, layouts, eye levels, in fact, test everything.

Watching your own business is often considered a luxury, especially for business owners. You suffer from the classic leadership conundrum of spending too much time working 'in' the business rather than working 'on' our business.

If you owned a pub, how comfortable would you be just to observe how your customers act, notice how often they drink, listen to what they ask for and be aware of their needs? I'm sure you'd be very comfortable with that, but the chances are you don't own a pub, so what's your equivalent?

And now for the easy part – take some action.

37

The customer is always right – not!

There's an old expression that says 'the customer is always right'. Is it true? Of course not. Customers get it wrong all the time and sometimes that can be to the detriment of you and your organisation. On those occasions you need to know how to react.

When my son was at university, during weekends and holidays he worked for a well-known retailer that (at that time) offered a fantastic 16-day money-back deal if you are not completely satisfied with the products. We had many conversations about customers bringing things back outside the 16-day policy and asking for a refund. There's nothing wrong with the product, they just changed their minds and left it a little too late.

Would it be five star service just to turn a blind eye to the advertised 16-day policy and give customers their money back on the 17th, 18th or 19th days? I don't think so. This organisation has a very clear method of trading and does it very successfully. However, the way in which you tell a customer that they can't have the money back in this particular instance is very important.

The **last thing they want to hear** are words like 'It's company policy' or 'I don't make the rules'.

But at the same time they do need to be told that there is a rule in place. Sometimes there are customers who will exploit the situation given the opportunity to do so, and they will continue to take more and more. You've heard the adage 'Give them a finger and they'll want your hand. Give them your hand and they'll want your arm. Give them your arm and you'll have nothing left.'

So how do you let customers know that **you're not a 'soft touch'**

but at the same time make them feel as though they have had **five star service**?

I believe it's about communicating in a clear, empathetic way with certainty and belief in your voice. Did you have a teacher at school who scared the living daylights out of you and if they told you to have your homework in by Wednesday morning, you did it mainly out of fear? You probably didn't like the teacher but you did as they said. Did you also have a teacher who would ask you to have your homework completed on time, but if you didn't it wouldn't really matter? I bet you liked that teacher! And I bet you had one or two teachers (a rare breed) who would ask you to have your homework completed by Wednesday morning, you did it, *and* you liked the teacher.

What qualities did they have that made you do as you were told and still they remained likeable? My guess is they believed in what they were doing and this came across in their manner. So if you do have to deliver news to a customer that they might not want to hear, make sure you believe in what you are saying first, then do it in a polite but firm way, and if they still don't like what you say then skim to 'It's your best friend – the awkward customer' (see page 185).

There's a difference between confidence and arrogance that needs to be explored here. When you are confident you have a certain demeanour that in most cases is seen as attractive.

People like **confident people** and like to be guided and led by them.

Beware – arrogance is only a few degrees away from confidence but instantly turns people off.

The challenge is when you are 'trying' to be confident you can easily come across as arrogant. The key word here is 'trying'. Confidence needs to be a natural part of what you do rather than forced. So how do you do it?

Know your stuff. You get this in two ways: studying it and doing it. When you become an expert in your ways of working, your products, your methods and your systems, you automatically become more confident. But the big one comes when you do it. *Every time you use a tool or technique it becomes easier; the easier it becomes the more confident you become; the more confident you become, the more in control you feel.*

Sometimes it's very difficult to do all of those things at once but there is a short cut, and the next section features three of the most powerful words I have ever learned which will show you how. When you use these three words in the right way, you can defuse almost any situation and align your customers to your way of thinking. The three magic words are:

Feel

Felt

Found

Read in the next chapter how you can use those magic words in many difficult situations, including the one we started this chapter with.

38

Feel, felt, found

'**Feel, felt, found.**' Three magic words and the best 'aligning' technique I've ever heard. They work so well and are easy to remember. This technique works very well with situations that are outside your control; you can stay strong and you'll get people coming to your way of thinking. Here's why.

Imagine the situation. You have to listen to a customer who wishes to complain about something that you cannot do anything about. You could easily say, 'I'm sorry, but company policy dictates that I can't do anything about this' – if there was ever a way to upset a customer it has to be starting a sentence with 'company policy dictates'.

This is why 'feel, felt, found' works so well.

Let's start with 'feel'. Who wouldn't like somebody who appreciates how another person feels? It's an instant way to align with a customer and at the same time show empathy. Here is how you could use the word in a sentence, 'I'm sorry you feel that way' or 'I can understand how you might feel.'

Now let's take a look at the word 'felt'. Felt is a powerful word because it does two things. It appears that you are viewing the situation from an historic perspective. It shows that you have experience of this situation. That's where the last word, 'found', comes in.

'Found' makes you the expert.

When people have 'findings' it usually means they have done a huge amount of work and research, and that research has come up with a fact, solution or answer. When you share your findings with your customer, you demonstrate your expert knowledge and you also empathise with their emotions. Lovely, isn't it?

'Feel, felt, found' has a remarkable way of breaking down barriers and aligning customers to your way of thinking. Here are a couple of examples of how it can work in practice.

> **Customer:** 'You mean to tell me it's going to take two weeks for it to be delivered? I think that's ridiculous.'

You: 'I understand how you might feel. Two weeks does seem like a long time. And before I started working here I probably would have felt the same, but do you know what I found? Because all of our products are ordered directly from the manufacturer we always ensure that we have the latest model to give to our customers. I also found that carrying a large amount of stock doesn't give us the opportunity to offer you the lowest price on the very latest models. We found most customers would rather have the latest model at the very best price.'

or

Customer: 'This is the third time I've had to call you with the same problem. And every time I get through to a different person and have to explain it all over again.'

You: 'I understand that you must feel frustrated with this. If I had explained the problem three times, I'm sure I would have felt the same. I've found that if I hear the details directly from our customer I am able to understand the issues more clearly and resolve the problem more rapidly, rather than reading some notes from a computer screen.'

And finally, from the previous section, what do you do when a customer is outside an already very generous returns policy and there's nothing wrong with the product?

Customer: 'I'd like a refund on this.'

You: 'I'm very sorry, but we are unable to give a refund outside of our 16-day satisfaction guarantee.'

Customer: 'That's terrible, it's only day 18. What difference does a couple of days make?'

You: 'I understand that you may feel unhappy about that and I have had other customers who have felt the same. But we've found that our satisfaction guarantee is one of the most generous in the high street and we've also found that the vast majority of people are delighted with it and can easily get back to the store in 16 days.'

Final thought:

If you're not sure this will work for you then I understand why you might feel that way. In fact before I actually tried it, I felt the same, but once I tested out the idea I found it worked brilliantly!

39

I honestly
don't care
about your
problems

A **new restaurant opened** in our local town. There was lots of publicity about the fantastic décor and background to the business. It was going to be the best place to eat and it would bring customers from the city. Fine dining like this on our doorstep was going to be wonderful.

Understanding that sometimes great restaurants take a couple of weeks to get into the swing of things, we avoided the opening night and the month that followed. So when the night of our booking arrived we were really looking forward to going out.

Other than the décor, which was really lovely, the night was a disaster. Warm (very expensive) white wine. Poorly cooked (very expensive) food. And staff who would have benefited from more thorough training. At the end of the night we noticed some friends of ours at a nearby table and joined them for a nightcap. Their experience had been similar to ours. Then, as luck would have it, one of the owners came to our table and asked how our night had been. This was one of those terrible choice moments: do you make someone feel better and say 'fine' or do you simply tell the truth?

We told her the truth. The lady listened, she nodded, said she understood and thanked us for the feedback. She said she hoped we would give them a second chance and return to the restaurant.

It was nice to have been listened to.

On the way out we met the other owner of the restaurant. Once again we were asked how our evening had been. This time we suggested he talk to his colleague as we'd just been through the whole story with her. But no, he insisted that we told him right there and then, every detail. He listened, shook his head and then went on to tell us a whole bunch of problems he was having. He griped about the supply of the wine, he blamed his staff (some who were just teenagers) and then he hit us with a classic. He explained that he was 'two chefs down' and one had walked out on him on Valentine's night.

At that moment I didn't care about why he had problems. I was **more**

interested in what he **planned** to **do** about them.

Here was a chap with a perfect opportunity to apologise, offer us a gesture of goodwill and ensure we returned to his restaurant to give him the opportunity to 'wow' us the next time. He could have made a new 'best friend'. He could have put a big deposit in our emotional bank accounts, but instead he took a withdrawal and with several hundred restaurants within easy driving distance we made our decisions and haven't been back.

How could he have improved our customer experience? Here's a simple list of do's and don'ts.

What *not* to say and do

Our system is down.

I tried but ...

We're having a staffing problem.

We've been very busy.

We can't do that because ...

Our policy is ...

The rules are ...

What to say and do

Thank you for your feedback.

We learn from what our customers tell us.

From what you have said we could be a lot better.

I'd like to make it up to you.

I'll make sure the right people get that feedback and we'll all learn from it.

I'd like to [fill in with something amazing] for you right now to win back some of your trust.

Then Wow them!

40

It's your
best friend –
the awkward
customer

You're doing a great job. You've done all you can and every-thing is sweet. Then suddenly it happens, the awkward customer appears. You know the one: they take hours of your time. They ask what seem to be the dumbest questions and change their minds constantly. No matter what you do, you can't seem to please them.

In *Fawlty Towers*, the brash owner Basil Fawlty dealt with customers, especially the awkward ones, in a unique way. He would scream and shout, and sometimes even physically remove them. He would treat his staff in the same way, and how we laughed. The temptation to 'do a Fawlty' is huge when Mr or Mrs Awkward is once again trying to make your life a misery, but you can't treat your customers that way. Shame ... but you can't.

Often the awkward customer has had something happen to them before you ever have the pleasure of dealing with them. It's rarely the fault of the person who is taking the wrath from this particular individual; however, they still get it double-barrelled, full on and with little consideration. This type of customer makes huge withdrawals from the emotional bank account (see page 49) of the unfortunate person who has to deal with them.

So what can you do?

Number one – you've got to listen. People love to be listened to, and awkward people really love it. Often they haven't been heard, so a good dose of listening can sometimes be all the awkward customer requires to get them 'on side'. Whatever you do, don't listen to that ridiculous advice about maintaining eye contact with the awkward customer. When you continuously maintain eye contact with somebody, it can be quite disturbing – for both parties. The best way to show you are actually listening is to nod, repeat key pieces of information (at the right time) to show you've understood, and put your head slightly on one side.

They all help, but the **very best way** to show you are **actively listening** is to **take notes**.

It's amazing that when you take notes, people understand that you are taking notice. In most cases, that's what the awkward customer really needs to believe, that somebody is taking notice.

Number two – empathise.

This of course can be very difficult. Try using language like, 'that's awful', 'I'm really sorry about that' and then suggest a way to help. Often poor customer service operatives end up asking, 'What would you like me to do about it?' Don't do this as it is antagonistic and can often make the situation worse. As *the expert, you should know exactly what you can do about it.* Offer a couple of suggestions before you give the customer an opportunity to tell you what they would like. For example, 'Would you like a replacement product?' Followed by 'Or is there something else I can do for you right now?'

But what if they just need to 'vent' for a while? Let them. Some people have a strong human need for significance. When these people come along, let them have their moments of significance by allowing them to have a huge download. Remember, what you don't have to do is take on board their negativity. In fact, you can turn it into a real positive moment – if you know how.

You mustn't feel you have to take the blame for somebody else's problems, particularly when you feel you've done everything you can within your power to make sure that their customer experience is five star. Remain calm and relaxed and in control. This sounds crazy but remember to breathe; if you stop you get stressed very quickly. Stay creative and solution orientated to ensure you do the right thing during those stressful situations.

Bonus Bit

The next time you have a really awkward customer who just wants to give you a hard time; even when you know you haven't done anything wrong and they just keep on going; even when you listen correctly, say 'that's terrible' and offer them two solutions and the chance to come up with their own solution and if they still keep going – then self-preservation is required.

Picture them naked. See them getting smaller and smaller, and in your mind give them a strange, high-pitched, squeaky voice. This last-resort technique can be used to protect you from other people's negativity and reduce stress too.

Wee Wow™

Three immediate actions to communicate bad news brilliantly:

1 Say sorry and mean it.
2 Offer a positive solution.
3 Follow up to make sure your customer is happy.

PART 6

Lessons in leadership

To be a service leader you don't have to be the boss, but if you are the boss you had better be brilliant at service leadership.

41

Who wants to fly with Captain Denny?

You've worked hard, your career is progressing well and congratulations — you deserve it. But is this meteoric rise taking you away from your customers? Should you worry? Should you do something about it? And if so, what?

Easy. Model Captain Denny Flanagan.

I was introduced to Captain Denny by Anthony Williams with this instruction: 'Michael, if you are writing about customer service, you *must* feature Denny Flanagan.' Captain Denny is a highly regarded, long-serving pilot with United Airlines with so many flying hours under his belt he could choose to just take it easy and leave Cabin Crew and Ground Staff to do the direct customer service work. But he doesn't. In fact, he's a brilliant example to all of his team in how to look after customers.

I was excited to find out more, so I wrote to him and asked whether he would like to join our mission! Here are a few extracts of what he sent back to me.

Dear Mr Heppell,

Thank you for reaching out to me. I looked you up on Google and was quite impressed with your accomplishments and I will take you up on your offer to help spread the word about just treating people NICE.

If employees only realised that their paycheck comes from the customers walking thru our doors then they would be more positive coming to work in the morning. I'm working from the bottom up but the effect is still contagious. There is a genuine dire need to satisfy our customers by some employees and we have developed a bond and the group is growing.

In the service business the recipe for success is quite easy. Anticipate your customers' needs and exceed their expectations. I have a few work philosophies and they have proved effective over the years:

Treat each customer as if it is their first flight and have no expectations ... I lead by example and this helps motivate the crew to do a better job. When they (the other staff) see me stow bags, assist moms with strollers and answer a question as if it is the first time I heard it they are brought back to their new hire days.

It is easier to keep the customers you have than to find new ones … United has a devoted sales team to find new customers and it is time-consuming and expensive but necessary. My job is somewhat easier and less expensive and that is to provide a safe and customer-oriented service. If I do my job then the folks in the Sales Department will have less pressure on themselves.

I have an array of ideas to connect with my customers and I keep them in my mental tool box. I'm constantly adding ideas and the tool box never gets heavier but my job just gets easier.

For years I have written notes to everyone in First Class, including employees. Customers I thank for their business and employees for their personal and professional effort because it makes a difference for all of us at United Airlines. I would also randomly send 20-plus cards to customers in coach.

I loved those ideas from Denny but my favourite was this:

On Fridays and Mondays the aircraft is predominately filled with business travellers who normally get the aisle or window seats. Many passengers have to sit in the middle and it is quite uncomfortable. The window and aisle customers claim the armrest and for the next few hours there is the strategic movement of arms to claim the coveted armrest. Your seat-mates may not even talk to you because that will reveal their nice side and then they will have to offer you their territorial claim.

My latest tool/idea is an attempt to make the middle seat psychologically and physically larger for my customers. For about two years I have written notes to the middle-seat customers on Mondays and Fridays. When the flight attendant leans over and says, 'Mr Heppell, I have a note for you from the Captain', two things happen. Emotionally your seat just got bigger because you were recognised by the captain. Physically your seat became bigger because your seat-mates move a bit to the right and left because now they want to know all about you and be your best friend. And now you have both armrests for the rest of the flight and they are talking to you.

Wow! Who wants to fly with Captain Denny?

Me! Me! Me! I know most of you don't fly planes, but what's your equivalent of making your customers feel amazing, important and loved?

Last year I received a brilliant email from Captain Denny. He was

due to be stopping over in London that night and hoped we may have time to meet up. I live 300 miles from London but I would have jumped on a train, plane or hitched a lift to get there. As it happened, I was staying in a hotel just 5 minutes away.

It shouldn't have been, but meeting with Captain Denny was a little scary. Here's a guy who I've held up as the perfect example of someone in a senior position who still delivers world-class service at the grass roots.

I needn't have worried. Denny is charming, entertaining and gracious. He told us about his mission and shared some other brilliant examples of what service leaders do.

Two really grabbed me.

While he was on the runway doing his pre-flight safety check before flying over to the UK, he saw a member of the ground crew bend over and pick up a piece of rubbish.

He immediately left the cabin and rushed down the steps. As he approached the guy, Denny noticed him quickly cover up his name badge. All Denny wanted to do was thank him for picking up the rubbish; 'As a pilot you're aware of all sorts of problems which can be caused by debris.'

Denny asked why he covered his badge and the response from the ground crew worker summed up the challenge he (and many others) face every day. 'When I saw you coming towards me, I guessed I must be in trouble for something. That's the only reason one of you guys would come down to talk to me.'

Denny thanked him for picking up the rubbish, for being part of the team and insisted on taking his name — to pass on to his boss what a fine team member he had.

And here's one to get your emotions going.

When Captain Denny holds his pre-flight team meeting, he asks the crew whether they have any 'unaccompanied minors' on board. If they do, Denny gives a strict instruction.

'Let's make sure they have the best flying experience ever. Make it VIP all the way. And can you give me their names and contact telephone numbers please. I'm going to call their parents from the cockpit and let them know their kids are safely on board and about to have a great flight.'

My wife asked Denny how the crew reacted to that. He said, 'Christine, I don't mean to make them cry, but you know your crew gets it when they shed a little tear.'

Who wants to fly with Captain Denny!!!

Wee Wow™

Just when you don't think it can get any better, here's how he finished his original letter to me:

'Michael, statistics reveal that for every compliment or complaint received, there are 100 others *thinking* of doing the same thing. Receiving your note from another continent brings joy to my heart that my positive efforts are spreading. Thank You.'

Capt. Denny

330-***-**** (My cell, in case you have any issues with United that I can assist with).

WOW!

42

Heads up!

Don't you just love the meerkat? An animal who in the last few years has emerged from relative obscurity to become one of the most widely loved mammals. They look cute, live in communities, eat snakes and weigh less than two pounds.

But did you know that meerkats teach their young the same way humans do? They can be observed demonstrating what to do, encouraging them to have a go, pointing out their mistakes then encouraging them to improve.

And did you know that a meerkat cannot produce body fat, which means they have to find fresh food to eat every day? And, because they are tasty, they have to be very careful when hunting so as not to become the hunted.

What can we learn from the lovable meerkat?

The meerkat's life isn't unlike that of the five star service professional.

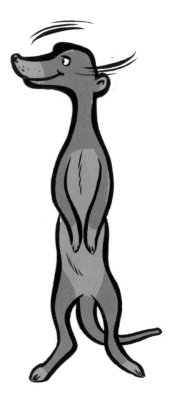

Perhaps the most distinctive member of the meerkat community is the 'lookout'. He is charged with two tasks: looking out for threats and searching for opportunities. His 'heads up' approach means he doesn't miss a trick.

Here's a big question, which requires a really honest answer. Do you work with your head up or head down?

It's easy to keep your head down and miss the odd opportunity to serve or problem to solve.

Here's how you can use 'heads up' to improve your system. Treat this as a game and make it fun:

Heads up instructions

Print a pile of cards with a picture of a meerkat on them. The cheesier the better!

Then give two cards to each team member.

During the next 7 days the goal is an easy one. You must give your two meerkat cards to two colleagues and tell them why you think they have demonstrated a *Heads Up* approach.

This sounds simple, but the psychology behind Meerkat Cards is what makes them work.

First of all you create a mini-culture, even if it's only for one week, where colleagues are looking for the positives about each other. Think about that for a moment: a whole organisation focusing on what's right rather than what's wrong.

Next, when a card is handed over, the recipient is told why. It may be that some people have done the same great work for years and they've never been recognised for it. Or it could be a one-off and recognition will encourage them to repeat it. Either way, I don't know anyone who is receiving too much recognition, do you?

And what about the person who, after a few days, still hasn't received a single card? We've witnessed team members creating opportunities to be given a card, telling others what they've done. In the past they may have been too modest to share, so it's all positive.

We used this system with an NHS Hospital Trust and received extraordinary feedback. Some porters on a couple of wards were occasionally a little tardy. Picking up a patient who needs to go from the ward to theatre is important, but to some porters being a few minutes late was neither here nor there. Of course, the challenge was the knock-on effect. Imagine a theatre team all gowned up and ready to go, but with no patient.

Bring on the meerkat cards.

When a porter arrived early to take a patient to theatre, nursing staff on the ward gave a Meerkat Card along with a few words of thanks.

After only a few days, porters began to arrive early and with a smile they asked, 'Am I getting one of those cards then?'

So for the cost of a small printed Meerkat Card, savings were made in lost theatre time. Colleagues were happier, but most importantly, patients were receiving a greatly improved service.

Think like the meerkat. The meerkat is always looking for **threats** and **opportunities** – you should do the same.

43

Recruiting service professionals

Hope is not a strategy when it comes to recruiting staff with a great service ethic. In fact neither are most of the diagnostic tools that may assess many things, but rarely predict how great staff will be with customers.

I remember once watching a programme in America called *The Rebel Billionaire*. It was a show a bit like *The Apprentice* but it featured Richard Branson in his quest to find someone to take over running part of Virgin. In the first episode the 16 young rebels flew in from the States, bright-eyed and ready to take on any challenge. They arrived in groups of four and were picked up in a London black cab. A film crew was on hand to capture them climbing into the cab, then, unbeknown to them, a secret camera recorded their journey to Branson's house.

So far so good – you couldn't have messed it up already? Could you? At this point you haven't even arrived at the interview.

The first thing they failed to notice was the elderly taxi driver and how he was struggling with their cases. Did they stop and offer to help? No, in fact a couple of the blokes let the girls struggle too.

Next was the conversation they had in the cab. Granted, the old taxi driver was egging them on by asking what they thought of Sir Richard but it was amazing how freely they shared their views, positive and negative, with a complete stranger.

Once they had all arrived, they met in the lounge and waited expectantly for their introduction to Sir Richard. Silence ensued as they did their best to look cool and professional. After all you get only one chance to make a first impression.

It was amazing to watch their mouths open when in walked not Sir Richard but the old taxi driver, who proceeded to stand up straight, change his voice and tear off his bulbous nose. Yes, you guessed it: the taxi driver was in fact a brilliantly made-up Sir Richard Branson.

He went on to show them some video clips of their behaviour since arriving at the airport, which left several of them red-faced. For one participant, who had made a particular idiot of himself, it was time to use the return portion of his ticket.

When it comes to recruiting service professionals you must **recruit on values** and **attitude first**.

Skills can be taught quickly, attitude takes longer and personal values are developed over years. I think you know the sort of attitude (or attributes) and values I mean: energetic, polite, caring, clean, timely, etc.

Here's a simple grid to help you decide, following your first encounter, where a person may fit with your five star service culture. It's not the most scientific approach but by scoring 1-10 and plotting where they land you may find yourself a gem.

HIGH		
	Can this person change?	HIRE THEM NOW!
Skills	Thanks but . . . no thanks	Give them a chance to learn the skills
	LOW Attitude & values **HIGH**	

The actual interview process (I think) is simple. Mainly because in an interview you have almost certainly made up your mind in the first few minutes and you then spend the rest of your time justifying your decision!

HR professionals may disagree. Here's what Liz McGivern, HR director of the multi-award-winning Red Carnation Hotel Group, says about what to look out for when interviewing service professionals.

First, I wouldn't say *don't* listen to your instincts as some people have good ones! I would say, don't *only* rely on them! A slightly more scientific approach could involve the following:

1   Ask yourself when you meet the candidate and during the interview, **what outlook or attitude does the candidate have**, particularly when you first meet and shake hands? (Is the candidate a natural smiler, friendly, who makes good eye contact with you? Or perhaps an extrovert and clearly interested in the job?)

2   These are all great pointers on how that person would be with your guests so take note and see whether you can picture them working for you. Remember even if they are nervous (and you can allow for nerves to an extent for some of your entry-level positions) **you are seeing them at their very best**. You could be compromising if you settle for less than these personality traits.

3   Asking questions on past experience is useful though you must ensure you are looking for actual episodic memories in the candidate's answers and not what I call 'textbook' or hypothetical answers. For professional service positions I like to **ask questions about a time they have dealt with a complaining and possibly angry guest**. What had happened? What did he or she say to calm the guest down? How did the guest respond to them and what did he or she offer to do for the guest? What was the outcome? Someone who handed the problem over immediately to their supervisor may not be able to act on their own initiative. On the other hand you may hear a brilliant story of how your candidate thought of and did all sorts of things to ensure the guest went away happy.

4   Other questions I ask for service positions could include **an unusual request and how they dealt with it**; a time they had to make a last-minute change; **a time they had to break the policy or procedure (or at least bend it a bit!) to give better service**; his or her best sale; a time when

they turned a negative situation into a positive one. Answers that are based on actual situations candidates have been in are revealing and helpful to you and indicate how someone is likely to behave in the future.

5   Last, whenever possible, invite **someone in for a trial day, or morning, or hour**! It's a two-way street for potential employee and employer. Remember, again, that as the employer, you are seeing the person at their best for the time they are with you.

So whether you're a professional recruiter or someone who just needs a part-time pair of hands, your intuition is the most important part of the process. Ignore it and you may just end up with second best.

44

Be individual, encourage individuals

I am not an airline snob as I just want to get from A to B in the quickest and most convenient way, so when low-cost no-frills airline easyJet started to fly out of my local airport I was thrilled. As my dad said, 'In business you never make money faster than when you're saving it' (it sounds perfect if you read that with a deep 'dad-like' voice in your head).

On an easyJet flight from London to Newcastle I had one of the best experiences I have ever had. Why? Because of Simon. Simon is the type of air crew you would love to headhunt for your organisation – even if the only purpose was pure entertainment value. He turned a dull 45-minute trip into a memorable experience. How did he do it?

From the moment we stepped on to the plane Simon had a different way of welcoming almost every person. He knelt down to greet the kids, he bowed respectfully yet humorously at two Japanese businessmen and, as I boarded, he said, 'I'd love to help you with your bag, but you look much stronger than me.'

But Simon came into his own once he got hold of the microphone. In a wonderful perky voice he announced, 'Welcome to this easyJet flight to Geordieland.' Most people cheered, although there were one or two groans. Quick as a flash he said, 'Don't worry, we will get the Mackems home too' (Mackems are people from Sunderland, Newcastle's big rival city 15 miles away).

He then went on to say, 'Please put all items in the overhead lockers. The only things that should be on the floor when we take off are your feet and the carpet.' This was closely followed by my favourite, 'Please turn off any electrical items, especially mobile phones, as they could interfere with the aircraft's navigation systems. The last thing we want to do tonight is end up in Carlisle.'

Once we were off the ground the cabin crew did a quick drinks trolley run where Simon offered everyone a 'cocktail of their choice'. The chancer sitting next to me asked whether he could have a pina colada. 'No problem at all, sir. But it may taste like lager and tonic.' And once again everyone howled with laughter.

When we landed at Newcastle Simon was ready for his grand finale and did the whole landing welcome in the style of Lily Savage. I had to write it

down as it was so good. Get a hard Liverpudlian accent in your head and read on, it went a bit like this: 'Hello, ladies and gentlemen, and welcome to Newcastle. Please don't even think about getting out of your seats until the plane has come to a complete standstill and that light has gone off. I'm watchin'. Please be careful taking any items out of the overhead lockers because after a landing like that they're bound to have moved!

'It's cold and damp in Newcastle tonight – for a change – so be careful as you go down the steps as they could be a bit slippy, love. Please make sure you take all items with you but don't worry if you forget anything because me and the girls are going to a car booty on Sunday and we're looking for a bit of extra tat. We realise that you have a choice of airlines. I can't believe you chose easyJet but as you did I have to say on behalf of all the crew, we appreciate your custom.' Then it happened. For the first time ever on a plane that hadn't been saved from certain disaster by a brave pilot, everybody burst into applause.

Simon created magic moments for everyone on the plane and judged the humour level brilliantly. Since the first edition of this book, lots of videos have appeared online. Could you be next?

You don't have to be just like Simon.

But let's take a quick look at what he did and what you can do too:

1 Know your customers – he had a different way to welcome most people on to the plane.

2 Know your product – he'd obviously made his announcements dozens of times and knew what he was doing. This gave him the confidence to do his extra material.

3 Local (or specialist) knowledge – he knew the local terminology for the people who lived in the major cities, he knew about the reputation Newcastle has for being cold, he knew what he had on his drinks trolley.

4 Get everyone involved. It is great to create a five star moment for an individual but to do it for over 100 people – that's special.

5 Use humour. Don't you just love to laugh too?

45

Restoration team

Do you remember watching TV when a home makeover show meant they would redecorate a room, tidy a garden or (at a push) titivate a pensioner's bungalow?

Well that's all changed. As I write, if you flick around your TV channels you'll quickly find revolutionary restoration, refurbishing and rebuilding projects that take 'makeover' to a whole new level.

I saw one recently (Extreme Makeover USA) where they built a brand new 5-bedroom house for a veteran's family, constructed a hurricane-proof village hall, refurbished 50 houses and converted a school — in a week!

On the other side of the coin there's *Restoration Man* and *Grand Designs*, where intrepid DIY enthusiasts take 5 years to convert a disused tram shed into their forever family home with a budget of £50k (and by the way they always go over budget).

Restoring service

If you have a service black spot, a shop that is underperforming, a regional office that gets loads of complaints or a pub with dodgy reviews, then you have a choice.

You can take a DIY approach; make small improvements in the hope that the small changes will add up over the years. Or go extreme!

Actually, there's probably something a little more appropriate some-where in the middle.

Let's take the best bits of the TV makeover format and see how they can be used in your business.

1 **Identify the need** In the TV shows the homeowners are usually nominated. Don't wait for a nomination. You know where you have challenges. Your customer satisfaction scores tell you, your intuition screams at you and the till doesn't lie.

2 **No surprises** The TV shows like to whisk the homeowner away for a weekend in Torquay so they can surprise them with a new garden on their return. You're not in TV so forget that. The

rule is — NO SURPRISES. Let the department, site, store, etc. know that you and/or a crack team will be coming to spend a few days/week/whatever with them. When you (or your crack team) first visit, take in the set-up, experience the process and meet the staff in their working environment.

3   **Work with the willing** On the TV shows they always have the family friend/colleague/daughter as part of the programme. They're usually the one who nominated the homeowner for the show and they'll have a backstory about what wonderful people they are (cue emotional music) and how their Mom ' ... really, really deserves this'. Two minutes later they're dressed in a pair of overalls, paintbrush in hand while Laurence Llewelyn-Bowen gives them a crash course in stippling, distressing a dresser and bedroom basics. This isn't about telling people what to do. It's about showing them first, then letting them do it themselves. Remember, this is restoration. Taking something that's well below par and making it great again. They need to care.

4   **A moment of truth** Every makeover show has a moment of truth. It could be discovering a stunning 1800's fireplace behind a wardrobe or giving an ambitious teenager a better place to study. It's a quick win and it symbolises why you're doing what you're doing. When you're doing a service restoration, you need one or two *ah ha* moments every day to spur the team on.

5   **Quick fixes and structural change** Your average makeover show isn't going to start taking out walls and rerouting a sewage system (although in America ...) so it's worth spending a little time working out what you can do: now, later on and never. **Now** is obvious. If you can change it now and it will improve the customer experience then get on with it.

Later on is important, but you probably aren't going to make it right in a week. However, you can schedule it. Take the first steps. Do SOMETHING to push the peanut forward. **Never**. Some changes are just too unrealistic. Choose your battles. Even the TV shows with their massive budgets can't change everything. Be realistic. Sometimes a workaround is useful, (see 'RADAR thinking™' on page 125 for some ideas on this). Remember, when you leave you want the team to feel encouraged and on a *journey* of change.

6   **Stay in touch and the follow up** I watched Kevin McCloud revisit some of his *Grand Designs* recently. The restorers were delighted to see Kevin; they wanted to show off and reveal how their houses had matured and become their homes. If you get it right and you send in experts who care rather than condemn, create rather than criticise and work together rather than take over, then you'll have set up a partnership.

Sizzling Pubs are a company who use this method. A refurbishment is as much about a revamp for the staff as it is about doing up the décor.

Rachel Lee, Guest Services Training Manager, told me, 'Each project has a dedicated trainer that delivers two days of service training. It's an opportunity that allows us to refocus the team and reignite a passion for service'.

Their results speak for themselves. A 21 per cent average weekly uplift in sales and a net promoter score increased from 71 per cent up to 87 per cent. Wow! Worth a two-day blitz? I think so.

5 Star Service restoration is about inspiration, giving staff a boost, showing them that you care and that you want them to enjoy their work more. The results of an intervention can be amazing. And if you do it really well, your talent pool of makeover professionals grows as the students become the teachers.

46

Ring the
bell

Here's a simple but effective idea to promote five star thinking and working in your organisation. And all it needs is a desktop bell. The basic idea is simply to encourage each other to ring the bell every time you have carried out a good customer service act or when you have something to celebrate.

I've used this idea for years and, in some organisations where we introduced it, it's become a major feature of their ways of working. It developed because I wanted people to share their successes.

I was working with a company and discovered that a salesperson had just completed a £10 million deal that day. He arrived back in the office, sat at his PC and sent an email to his boss, who the next morning sent a reply saying 'well done'. He was to be congratulated at the annual recognition event that was taking place six months later.

So I started to think. We've all been to similar events. They are great fun and very motivational, but what about the other 360-plus days of the year? How do we celebrate success then? I'd had a bell on my desk for years and would use it to create a 'ding' for my team, but there was nothing formal behind it. The following week I was back with my client and I gave them my bell. We set some rules for what you had to do in order to 'ring the bell'. *Most people could qualify to ring the bell at least once per day.*

Then something really brilliant happened. The first person to ring the bell sheepishly walked up to the desk it was on and gave it a ting. Three or four of her colleagues gave a little cheer, then she was asked the question (which really makes this system work), '*What have you done?*' She then went on to tell a 15-second story of how she prevented a customer from switching to a competitor and saved the company a few thousand pounds.

She was talking about **best practice.**

She was **getting recognition.**

She was creating a **feel-good** atmosphere in the office.

So picture the scene. You are part of a team of 15 people working in an open-plan office and perched right in the middle of all the desks is your celebration bell. Then:

Decide what will be the criteria for ringing the bell.

Make sure everyone celebrates when someone rings the bell – even just a little 'wahoo' is better than a stony silence.

Keep reinventing the idea and make it fresh.

There's one other secret bonus of using the bell technique to celebrate and promote success. What would happen if you hadn't rung the bell for a few days and all your colleagues had? Wouldn't it drive you on to want to ring it?

It really does spur people on to ring the bell on a regular basis – every 'ting' is a successful thing!

Actions

Five-step guide to ringing the bell:

1 Buy a bell (or a bunch of them).
2 Place it in a prominent position in the room.
3 Decide on the rules for what you have to do to ring the bell (let people break the rules if they have something to celebrate!).
4 Encourage people to ring the bell by asking, 'Have you rung the bell for that?' whenever you hear about a success. It takes a little while to create new habits.
5 Give people the freedom to tell their story of best practice and record as many of the exceptional ones as you can in your five star journal (see page 264).

Wee Wow™

I have one client who bought a gong to bash for anyone who really went the extra mile. They put it right next to the accounts department (a very challenging part of the company) so they would know exactly who was bringing in the money.

47
Service values

In my book *How to Be Brilliant* I wrote about Harry Nicolaides who worked as a concierge, and the truly brilliant influence he had on me and the guests of the Rydges Hotel in Melbourne. It is with deepest regret that I must inform you that Harry has moved on to live in Phuket, Thailand.

The last time I visited Melbourne I arrived in Rydges with an air of anticipation, wondering whether the experience would be the same without him. Within 30 minutes of arrival it hit me. Rydges was now another average hotel. Why? Brilliance was the culture of one or two individuals and not of the organisation as a whole. I was devastated! The first time I visited I was on my own, this time I had my family with me and I hadn't shut up about how amazing this hotel had been. Now that Harry had moved on, sadly the magic had left with him.

So how do you **create** a **five star culture** rather than relying on one or two individuals who make your organisation shoddy or **shine?**

Get the values right. Service values are critical to the success of any organisation. Make sure they are written down, widely distributed and most of all used. Without the right values system, how will you know whether you are creating a five star culture?

Almost all organisations have a mission statement or vision – it's usually written by a bunch of executives during an 'off-site meeting' in a large country house. Values are different. They need everyone to have an input because when you really live them (especially service values), decisions are easier, people are clear on their wider objectives and customers really feel them. *Is five star service a company value for you?*

Have you ever thought about arranging an internal training session to work on this? It can be as easy as getting a team together and asking everyone this key question: 'What was your best customer service experience and how much did it cost?' You'll soon notice that the very best customer service experiences have little or no financial cost. The next step is to ask what you have learned from people's anecdotes and which bits you can apply in your organisation.

Encourage some team members to take up the challenge (or do it yourself) and create posters, stickers and devices to promote the level of customer service you expect. *Celebrate success.* Read the chapter 'Ring the bell' (on page 215) about celebrating successes. This gesture makes everyone in an area look up. It encourages people to share success and, if you haven't rung the bell for a while, you'll do whatever it takes to make it ring!

You may be a service genius, your organisation may have two or three service superstars and that's great. But if you can't create a culture where five star service is a value and a standard, you and the other stars are going to become frustrated very quickly. So it is well worth the effort to get others involved.

Is it worth it? Well, we're living in times where customers demand more from less and they don't even tell you about it. You must be at the leading edge when it comes to creating outstanding five star customer service. Make it a must!

So how do you write a set of service values you can live by?

First of all, writing any set of values is as easy or as difficult as you'll want to make it. I've worked with companies that have done it in an afternoon and been very successful and I've worked with others that have taken months and barely got off the starting block.

I'm going to assume that you will be the champion of your organisation's company service values. Here's a simple system you can use.

Get everyone (or as close as you can) together. This is probably the single hardest task. You'll have to find a way to get maximum buy-in to the process and getting together the people who are going to be delivering the message is vital. If you can't, then find a powerful way to communicate what you are doing to the whole organisation. This needs to be more than a memo.

Introduce why you think having customer service values is important. Give some anecdotal evidence and share the benefits of values: freedom, compliments, ease of decision making, etc.

Now ask your team two questions: what is **important to them** and what do they think is **important to their customers.**

It's often a good idea to get small groups discussing these ideas rather than trying to take lots of feedback from a large group (if there are fewer than 10 people in your organisation, that's a perfect number to work with).

Look for themes

Look for themes running through the information given but be aware of not leading the group down a route they don't want to go. Identify words that can be used as values. Say you have three statements saying, 'Wow our customers', 'Make it feel new' and 'Be different'. Ask the group whether they think the word 'surprise' could sum that up. If they do, great; if not, ask why – and listen.

Key words

The next stage is to work towards getting a few key words that sum up your customer service values. Here's where it can get interesting because people often want to put the cart before the horse and know an exact description for a value before it goes on the list. That's when it takes weeks instead of hours, so tell the participants you'll come to that but right now you are looking for some key words to work on.

Prioritise

The next stage is to take what could be a long list and make it into a shorter one. The simple way is to look for similar words and chunk them. Then prioritise them and lose the bottom ones if it feels like you have too many (rule of thumb – if you can't remember the list you have too many).

Write descriptions

Then you write the descriptions. Again this could be done in small groups if you are a big team or as a whole. Descriptions should be short and concise and give a brief empowering description of the actions that go with the key words i.e. Accurate: We get it right every time.

Spread the word

When you've done all that make sure everyone knows them and knows how to use them and encourage everyone to sign up to them. Next print them out and stick them on the walls. Make small laminated cards with them on. Tell people to share moments when they use them – challenge the people who don't. Post them on your website (you can see mine at www.michaelheppell.com). Make them a part of your culture. This takes a little bit of time and may never be perfect but the effort pays back substantial rewards.

If you're stuck while brainstorming, here are a few ideas to get you started:

Brilliant	Accurate	Polite
Punctual	Magic	Creative
Fun	Thoughtful	Unique
Involved	Excellence	Referable
Genuine	Friendly	Fun
Best value	Motivated	Surprise
Second mile	Clean	Famous
Systematic	Consistent	Funky
Award winning		

48

Empowering staff

was asked to speak at a conference for the BBC at London Zoo. The event went well and we had an opportunity to sell books afterwards. My first book *How to Be Brilliant* had just been published and I was delighted when my team informed me that we had sold out (always good news for a first-time author).

I said my goodbyes and left to attend another event. Here's where a potential challenge occurred. Chris, the director of the department who had booked me, came over to the book stand, apologised for his delay and asked for a copy of my book. My team (by now one person) had to tell him that we'd sold out but we'd post one to him the next day. 'No problem,' he said, then turned to a colleague and said, 'Shame, that. I was going to read it on the plane in the morning.'

Here's where a bit of preparation and luck combine to create a brilliant five star service experience. My colleague was using 'heads up!' and heard his second comment, and then took action. Ten minutes later she was in a cab looking for a book store. Once she found a store she ran in and bought a copy of *How to Be Brilliant*. Next she jumped into another cab and was on her way to BBC HQ. When she arrived she persuaded security and the staff at Chris's office to allow her to place the newly purchased copy of the book on his desk with a handwritten note hoping he would enjoy *How to Be Brilliant* and have a safe flight.

A couple of hours later Chris arrived to pick up his papers ready for the following day. Wow! was his first expression. He couldn't understand how (a) we knew he was flying, (b) we knew he wanted a book for the flight and (c) a company based in Northumberland had managed to get a copy of *How to Be Brilliant* to him.

And guess who he told about this? That's right ... everyone!

So how did my colleague know she could spend the time, money and energy doing this and why did she bother? Easy, since the early days of Michael Heppell Ltd we have empowered our team with details of: how much money they can spend, how much time they can take and that whatever they decide to do must fit with our company values, to make sure we create amazing five star experiences for our customers. You *never* have to ask permission to do this, you just go for it and, even if you

make a spectacular mistake, that's perfectly OK. We present it as a triad to make it easy to recall.

At that time Michael Heppell Ltd staff could spend one hour and up to £50 to make a customer's experience memorable and, so long as it fits with one of our values, it's perfectly acceptable.

Taking the example of getting a book to Chris at the BBC, the formula worked perfectly:

- Total cost – £43.99 (taxis: £34, book: £9.99)
- Time – 50 minutes
- Values – Michael Heppell Value No.5 'Go the second mile and surprise'

Easy.

If you are the boss, ensure your staff know: **how much**, **how long** and the **spirit** (**values**) of what they are allowed to do.

If you are not the boss – ask yours to fill in the blanks.

How much money can your staff (or you) spend to make a customer's experience better? How much time can you devote? How will you know what to do and why?

Actions

Five things to do to empower five star service in your staff. If you don't have staff, ask your boss whether you can do these.

1 Set a budget – both in cash and time terms. It's amazing that people often don't take the chance to create an opportunity or fix a problem because they don't feel authorised to spend any of the organisation's money.

2 Share best practice. Create opportunities to share what others have done via awards/a notice board/a newsletter/team meetings, etc.

3 Look back at some 'live' examples of where people felt they weren't empowered and explore what would or could have happened if they had been.

4 Create a 'no fail' environment where, if someone should take an initiative and get it wrong, they haven't failed but instead they have had a big slice of learning.

5 Do it. Find opportunities to do it. Create opportunities to do it. Because the secret is not in the knowing, It's always in the doing.

PART 7

Business blueprint

Organisations who excel at customer service make more money and save more money. Need I say more?

49

Rate the brand

DECIDE. are 'decision architects' who specialise in helping companies to positively influence the decision making of consumers. With the thousands of decisions the average person is making every day, their job is to ensure savvy shoppers choose their clients' products over their competitors'.

And they are very good at it.

Their MD Jerry Hall told me, 'Customer service is brand experience.' I think I knew what he meant but I still asked for more.

He went on to explain.

A brand is more than a name or logo it's also a promise of an experience.

Every interaction between a person and brand is a brand experience and this can be through TV adverts or in-store. But it's also, online, on the telephone, or face to face, with employees and also other customers.

The growth of social media over the past few years has dramatically shifted power to the customer, with 'word of mouth' massively influencing buyer behaviour.

In fact, 'word of mouth' is the primary factor behind 20 to 50 per cent of all purchasing decisions, particularly for first-time buyers or expensive items.

This means your customers have decided what type of organisation you are, based on many factors intentional and unintentional, many of which you won't see in an organisation's marketing plan.

It also means you have a brilliant opportunity to do something about it.

When we work with companies, we often use games to get discussions started. One very popular game is called, 'Rate the brand'. The idea is simple; the results are outstanding.

We have 10 cards. Each has a well-known brand (logo) printed on it. For example we have Virgin, Microsoft, Ryanair, John Lewis, the NHS, etc.

The brief is simple, 'Arrange the cards from the best to the worst customer service brand.'

The group then get to work. Here's where it gets interesting. One person usually dives in, takes a card and says, 'They have to be at the top (or at the bottom).' Often the group will agree. There are always some service brands that leap out.

However, it's rare that a group will agree with all the top three or bottom three. And during that discussion as people fight for what they believe is true, you hear certain words and phrases come up again and again:

'That's not what I've found.'

'I love xx, here's why.'

'In my experience... '

On many occasions we have witnessed people defend or berate a brand so strongly that the rest of group just back down.

It's interesting to explore how groups have ended up with certain brands at the top and others firmly at the bottom.

But what's really fascinating is unpicking why.

Even though at no time during the briefing did we ask people to share their personal experience, everyone does. Having a strong personal 'Why?' overcomes any marketing, advertising or PR campaign.

Now here's a question for you to consider. If we added an 11th brand — yours, where would you end up?

50

★

Service
PR

What are you known for? Could you win a Customer Service Award?

When you completed the Service Star™ in Chapter 1 you'll have noticed one of the potential areas where you can score high marks is service PR. In simple terms this is what people are saying about you, often in the media but more so these days online, between customers and even within your own staff.

Some organisations spend fortunes with public relations companies, developing gimmicks and ideas to spread the word about their amazing (usually their words) service. Even with all that spend they still get poor results.

Others spend huge amounts trying to keep their lousy service reputation out of the public domain. You can imagine the scenario at the board meeting, budgets are being carved up and the big cheese is terrified in case he loses his 'defence PR budget'.

Then there are some who have plenty to shout about, use just the right amount of PR to fan the flames but leave the majority of their positive PR to their customers; loyal customers who are happy to rave about their experiences and defend the company wherever necessary.

So how do you go about creating fabulous service PR? Here are seven steps to get you started.

- **Step 1** (And this should be blatantly obvious) create fabulous five star service. I had a potential client who wanted to win a national customer service award, and asked me how I thought he should go about it. After I'd explained what I thought was necessary, he asked, 'Is there an easier way?'

- **Step 2** Make sure everyone in your organisation knows you want to create fabulous service PR. Again this seems glaringly obvious but you'll be amazed how many people want to keep their service sensation a closely guarded secret. Encourage your team to share successes, learning experiences and solutions to customers' challenges.

- **Step 3** Document what you do. Having a great story you can tell is good. Having it documented for others to read is brilliant.

- **Step 4** Share the success! Write a newsletter. Send out news releases. Employ a PR company. Fill your website with facts about how wonderful you are.

- **Step 4.5** Get over the fact that Step 4 didn't achieve much! Brilliant service PR takes a bit of time and needs something far more powerful than you shouting about how good you are. That's right, it needs your customers to shout.

- **Step 5** Give your customers something to shout about. In his brilliant and free eBook *Flipping the Funnel,* author Seth Godin talks about giving your customers a voice to promote you. Imagine what your service PR would be like if you could show your customers how to shout about you. This isn't something you can do by broadcasting. Start conversation with your customers. Use social media, pick up the phone, ask questions and listen.

- **Step 6** Get recognised. Enter your organisation for a national customer service or WOW award. You might just win. Or write to me about what you've achieved. I'm always happy to share examples of service success if I think it will benefit my readers and audiences.

- **Step 7** Be sure you can walk the talk. Promoting yourself as a five star service organisation means you can't hide behind inexperience, downturn, poor training, company policy or any of the other excuses you may have clung onto in the past.

Service PR can't be bought – or if it can it doesn't last.

Service PR comes from being able to genuinely **celebrate your service success** and have your customers do the same.

51

Sell me a solution

like Sky. I subscribe to sports, movies, documentaries, high definition, multi-room, everything really. So when it came to searching for a new broadband provider I looked at their offering of lightning speed and low cost (still waiting for the lightning speed here in rural Northumberland by the way) and ordered my new service.

The order process was a chore, but as a loyal customer I forgave them, just so long as they fulfilled their promise of the new product by Christmas. Then we had some delays, which I was able to overlook – as a loyal customer. Then the router etc arrived on Christmas Eve and only one of our computers worked (luckily mine, unluckily not the kids'). Can you imagine the horror of being a teenager without Facebook over Christmas?

Then the fun really started. For two weeks I had almost daily calls with a wonderful array of technical people. All were polite, helpful and patient. However, none of them managed to connect our laptops to the internet. Then, after various levels of 'escalation' I was eventually connected to a techie of such knowledge and standing I wouldn't have been surprised to hear that he had invented the internet!

His first question was, 'Are you using a wireless USB Sky dongle in your laptop?' I didn't even know there was such a thing as a Sky dongle, so I asked him where you got them from. He informed me that, 'Sky sell them, they are £20 each and can be delivered via a "next day" service.' Problem solved.

Here's what puzzled me. Why had I spent an average of two hours a day, three or four days a week for the past two weeks talking to the lovely patient people at Sky technical support, resetting IP addresses and goodness knows what else, when the problem could have been fixed for £20?

The solution was easy.

But why wasn't I offered this solution by any of the other many, many people I talked to? Because it would mean they had to ask for a sale, and many people have a limiting belief that asking for a sale doesn't always sit well with great customer service.

There are of course two sides to this argument, which can be answered with one simple question.

Will my customer be **better served** and **feel valued** if they have to **make a purchase** to find their **solution**?

Approached in the right way, and with the needs of your customer put first, most people are delighted to pay for a solution, if it offers real value. Here are some examples:

> You'd like 'at seat' service, wider seats and a comfy quiet journey? Then you'd buy a first-class ticket.

> You want to come in from work and find your ironing done and the house immaculate? Then you'd employ a housekeeper.

> You want your computer to work brilliantly, never crash and be able to store hours of video and millions of photographs? Then you'd buy one with a huge memory and a better processor.

Five star service **doesn't mean you can't charge more** for providing better value.

In fact, selling the solution may be the best way to create a brilliant customer experience.

52

Building a customer service brand

Brand, **brand, brand**. It's all about brands in the business news today. Who has the most recognised brand, whose is worth the most? How much money was spent on a new brand launch? When it comes to five star service there are no prizes for guessing how important the brand is – it's everything. Because at the end of the day, the brand is you. It's what you do on a regular basis that makes the difference.

At seminars I often ask, 'Who would like £100,000 to be invested in them?' All the hands shoot up. Then I show a slide, which says, 'You Ltd' and I ask if they were a company and I had £100,000 to invest in them, would they deserve the money? Again lots of hands shoot up. We all like to think we *deserve* the money. When I ask why they deserve the money, we have the key moment. Most people have no idea why and the hands start to drop. The ones who remain are asked to give a 15-second commercial as to why they should get the cash.

Their replies are varied. From the people who glibly offer to double my money (I still can't get them to put that in writing), to those who give a pitch as though they're a registered charity and before they've had a chance to whip out their violins they've usually run out of time. After four or five 'infomercials', I ask the group who they would invest in. In most cases I get a response which exemplifies what being 'brand you' is all about. It's the most likeable person who gets all the votes. Not the ones who 'deserve it', not the ones who insist they are a 'great investment', but the ones you would most like to be friends with.

And that's what customer service branding is all about – making **your service so good** that you end up being with **friends,** not just **customers.**

Kevin Roberts (the worldwide CEO of Saatchi & Saatchi) talks about 'lovemarks'. He describes them as 'the future beyond brands'. A love-mark takes loyalty to a whole new level where not only are you loyal to the brand, but you also actively promote it. You persuade others to switch, you feel like you are part of the family and you fight their corner. Most lovemarks are created by organisations that care about people first. Could you describe your organisation as one worthy of a lovemark?

BIG QUESTION

If the brand is all about **you**, **what** are you doing to grow '**brand you**'?

Actions

Here are five thoughts to grow 'brand you' and make your customers fall in love with yours truly:

1 Remember, you are the brand. It's just the company logo that goes on ads and stationery.
2 Brand needs constant rejuvenation. Never allow yourself a day off from being the very best you can be.
3 Brands are built on rock-solid values. Do you have values written down that you stand by every day?
4 Brands are borderless. Does what you do extend outside your immediate circle of influence? Could 'brand you' go international and still get top results?
5 Question why you are loyal to some brands and repelled by others. Take the parts that attract you and do them more, take the parts that repel you and do them less.

53

Hills and valleys

S you study these techniques you will notice that you go through several distinct stages of learning. There are five and I call them 'hills and valleys'.

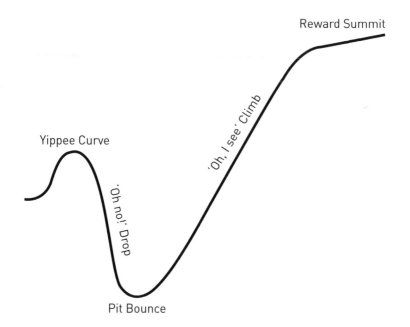

Reward Summit

'Oh, I see' Climb

Yippee Curve

'Oh no!' Drop

Pit Bounce

Yippee Curve

The first is the 'Yippee Curve'. The Yippee Curve is a great place to be because you start to use your new ideas and you get some amazingly quick results. In fact, you'll be so excited about using the ideas from 5 *Star Service* that you won't even notice if things go wrong. And if you're part of a team of people who are all using the techniques then the Yippee Curve will be even longer.

'Oh no!' Drop

The next stage is what I call the 'Oh no!' Drop. 'Oh no!' Drop is an interesting place to be because, even when you are using your tools and techniques that you've learned from this book, you still seem to get things wrong. This can be very frustrating but it's not unlike learning any new skill and being shown a new way to approach an old habit.

I once took some golf lessons and for the first few rounds afterwards my game hadn't improved at all. In fact, I was concentrating so much on the new tools and techniques that I'd learned from the professional that my game became worse. But it wasn't long before the investment in the new ideas started to pay off and I was able to hit the ball straight and further than ever before.

Pit Bounce

The next place is what I call 'Pit Bounce'. It may seem daunting but it's actually a great place to be – because as you get to the lowest point there's going to be a big bounce which will catapult you into the next stage. It's all about sticking with it. I see so many people quit because they've got to the pit and haven't realised that there's a bounce that's going to take them up, up, up. It can be a confusing place to be, but that's OK because the next stage is what I call the 'Oh, I see' Climb.

'Oh, I see' Climb

The 'Oh, I see' Climb is where it all starts to make sense and your hard work really begins to pay off. The techniques become easier and easier and five star service becomes a way of life. You really begin to fully understand the ideas and make them work even better for you, and by doing so you start to master the techniques.

Reward Summit

The final level is Reward Summit. This is where it all starts to pay off. You begin to reap the benefits offered by the ideas in this book and start mastering them.

Realising that you're going to progress through these five stages is an important part of implementing these ideas. In fact, if you don't go through all five stages I really believe you aren't going to get the best out of the learning process.

So when you get frustrated and some of the ideas appear not to be working as well as you had expected, recognise that you're probably going through an 'Oh no!' Drop, adjust your behaviour, take some positive action and celebrate the bounce.

Actions

Five things to do as you go through each stage:

Yippee Curve	Enjoy it! Make the most of every new tool and test them out.
'Oh no!' Drop	Recognise it and ensure you have people around you to support it – never ever quit.
Pit Bounce	Don't dwell. Rewrite your goals and make a decision to aim even higher.
'Oh, I see' Climb	Document your learning. As you realise how well you are doing, it becomes easier to apply the ideas and sometimes you forget how you got here.
Reward Summit	Teach other people what you have learned. Give something back.

54

Using 5 Star Service as a training resource

The first edition of 5 *Star Service* has been used by many people as a training resource as much as an inspirational book. Almost every day we receive emails and calls from people who have used or are using 5 *Star Service* with their staff.

Of course in a perfect world you would pick up the phone, call me and I'd be happy to come and present the ideas to you, but the reality is I can't be in two places at the same time (yet).

Ideas such as the Service Star™, RADAR thinking™, Wee Wows™ and the Spanners and Heroes game have become regular training activities for hundreds of organisations. I want more people to use 5 *Star Service* as a training aid so this chapter is designed to give you a framework to implement the ideas into your organisation.

To get the best out of this chapter and to make it fair for everyone I suggest we negotiate a learning contract. I'll tell you what I'll do and then I'll suggest what you should do. If we both agree then the resources are yours.

Here's what I'll do:

I will give you a suggested 90-day (13-week) framework to suit your organisation.

These ideas are listed because they've been tested and they work.

And here's the best bit. As you've bought this book, to say thank you I won't charge you anything for everything listed above.

Here's what I would like you to do:

Agree not to photocopy any part of this book. If you want more, please buy them (they are great value).

Credit the source for any of the materials you use. 'This is an idea from Michael Heppell's book, *5 Star Service*' would be perfect!

You won't charge anyone for using these materials. If you are unsure because you are a sub-contractor, trainer, coach or presenter then contact Michael Heppell Ltd (details are at the back of this book) and ask. We normally say yes when we are asked and we generally sue when we aren't.

I've created five programmes that cover:

Five star in the office

Five star for retail

Five star for hotels and restaurants

Five star for the public sector

Five star for education

If you don't fit with any of those then take a peep at the content of each and use it as an inspiration to create your own.

Here are the suggested plans with a few thoughts thrown in.

Five star in the office

Week 1   **The Service Star**™ Every programme starts here. It's how you know where you are and how you'll know when you're getting better!

Week 2   **Wee Wows™** An easy concept that gives you some quick wins.

Week 3   **Heads up!** Once you have explored the concept be sure to get the buy-in from everyone involved. Schedule a review in a month.

Week 4   **Ring the bell** If you are the leaders it is essential that you encourage people to ring the bell over the next seven days to create a success habit.

Week 5   **Super scripts and it's not what you say** This is very powerful for telephone service, dealing with internal customers and suppliers.

Week 6   **Systemise routines – personalise exceptions** Ensure you have a few examples up your sleeve to get the discussion started.

Week 7   **Empowering staff** You need to know that what you agree to in this session can be implemented immediately. So it's good to know your limitations and breadth of flexibility at this point too.

Week 8   **Complaints – a chance to shine** Be watchful during this session to keep it upbeat and avoid any kind of blame culture.

Week 9   **What's in a name?** Have a few ideas that you have worked out here. If you belong to a large organisation it can be fun to have a name quiz featuring pictures of people from other departments too.

Week 10   **RADAR thinking**™ As soon as you have completed this session take massive action to implement your ideas. Remember to schedule your review time in too.

Week 11 **Telephone service and advanced telephone service** Everyone 'thinks' they are getting the basics right but it's worthwhile reviewing them before you move on to the advanced techniques.

Week 12 **Top three referability habits** An easy one this week but don't be fooled by it. These three techniques need a good five minutes each to explore how you can do each one better.

Week 13 **Spanners and Heroes** Lots of fun, chaos and learning to be had on this your final week. This exercise can take up to one hour so, if you can, schedule some extra time.

Five star for retail

It's a tough time in retail so you have to be better than ever.

As customers demand more, you have an obligation to make every transaction magical.

Week 1 **The Service Star**™ Every programme starts here. It's how you know where you are and how you'll know when you're getting better!

Week 2 **Wee Wows**™ An easy concept that gives you some quick wins.

Week 3 **Heads up!** Once you have explored the concept be sure to get the buy-in from everyone involved. Schedule a review in a month.

Week 4 **The emotional bank account** Link this right up to the point where you ask a customer to pay, and explore how happy they would be to hand their money over if their 'account' with you is already overdrawn.

Week 5 **One chance to make a first impression** It can be easy to point out some of the things that are wrong with your team here but instead ask your team to point out who does each of the points well.

Week 6	**Empowering staff and secret shopper** If you are going to use the secret shopping techniques, then now would be a good time to introduce them. When it comes to empowering staff you need to know that what you agree to in this session can be implemented immediately. So it's good to know your limitations and breadth of flexibility at this point too.
Week 7	**Complaints – a chance to shine!** Be watchful during this session to keep it upbeat and avoid any kind of blame culture.
Week 8	**Big Buyer is watching you** For this session it is very powerful to have a personal example or two in mind so you can get the ball rolling. No one likes to think they are guilty of the challenges in this area so play it safe and allow lots of discussion.
Week 9	**RADAR thinking**™ As soon as you have completed this session take massive action to implement your ideas. Remember to schedule your review time in too.
Week 10	**It's your best friend – the awkward customer** This should be one of your most fun sessions with a serious message. It may be fun to hear some examples from your team of what they consider an awkward customer to be like.
Week 11	**99 per cent of people are good** I know you are probably tied by company rules and regulations here, but the idea is not to change the rules, it's to reframe how you handle them.
Week 12	**Sell me a solution** Get this right and you'll see confidence and profits soar! The idea is very simple, the application is not. Take time to role-play ideas and perhaps incorporate super scripts.
Week 13	**Spanners and Heroes** Lots of fun, chaos and learning to be had on this your final week. This exercise can take up to one hour so, if you can, schedule some extra time.

Five star for hotels and restaurants

Choosing just 13 sessions for you is a real challenge as you'll want to be brilliant at everything in this book. However, you have to start somewhere and this programme gives you a wide range of skills and some timely reminders of what you should be doing.

Week 1   **The Service Star**™ Every programme starts here. It's how you know where you are and how you'll know when you're getting better!

Week 2   **One chance to make a first impression** It can be easy to point out some of the things that are wrong with your team here but instead, ask your team to point out who does each of the points well.

Week 3   **Heads up!** Once you have explored the concept be sure to get the buy-in from everyone involved. Schedule a review in a month.

Week 4   **Wee Wows**™ An easy concept that gives you some quick wins.

Week 5   **Beware the silent customer** This week you can really play up the idea of outstanding five star service and creating advocates of your hotel or restaurant.

Week 6   **RADAR thinking**™ As soon as you have completed this session take massive action to implement your ideas. Remember to schedule your review time in too.

Week 7   **Customer magic moments** Read the chapter about Captain Denny Flanagan and how he treats every customer as if they are flying for the first time. This is a magical way to start your session.

Week 8   **The blind spot** I think you will be surprised at how many 'blind spots' you have when you start to discuss this issue. If someone shares an example, be sure not to ask, 'Why didn't you mention it?' and make sure you do say, 'Thank you.'

Week 9   **The distraction of dirt** Not an easy one but a vital one. There will be plenty of people who would like to hand over responsibility in this area to someone else. The secret is to make sure everyone feels like they can make a positive difference.

Week 10 **What's in a name?** Have a few ideas that you have worked out here. If you belong to a large organisation it can be fun to have a name quiz featuring pictures of people from other departments or shifts too.

Week 11 **Special requirements** The main purpose of this session is to change thinking from one of 'how inconvenient' to one of 'wow, our chance to shine'. Gather a few real-life examples first and use this session as a chance to educate.

Week 12 **It's not what you say** It's week 12 now and you should have the confidence to role-play a little and test out some of the ideas more thoroughly.

Week 13 **Spanners and Heroes** Lots of fun, chaos and learning to be had on this your final week. This exercise can take up to one hour so, if you can, schedule some extra time.

Five star for the public sector

Having worked with dozens of public-sector organisations including the NHS and regional police forces, I don't accept that it's a more difficult environment in which to create five star service. You just have to approach it in a different way. The programme I've outlined here should excite anyone who is committed to public service.

Week 1 **The Service Star**™ Every programme starts here. It's how you know where you are and how you'll know when you're getting better!

Week 2 **Wee Wows**™ An easy concept that gives you some quick wins.

Week 3 **Heads up!** Once you have explored the concept be sure to get the buy-in from everyone involved. Schedule a review in a month.

Week 4   **The emotional bank account** Public sector differs here as customers feel they have already 'paid' for their service. This means you often start from a place of withdrawal. Explore what that means.

Week 5   **Systemise routines – personalise exceptions** Ensure you have a few examples up your sleeve to get the discussion started.

Week 6   **RADAR thinking**™ As soon as you have completed this session take massive action to implement your ideas. Remember to schedule your review time in too.

Week 7   **What's in a smile?** This should provide you with lots of quick wins. I know you want to smile, I know you do smile, but public perception is often different. This is your chance to change that.

Week 8   **Super scripts** Scripts give continuity and the right script can effortlessly take a person from A to B. Whether it's on the phone, face to face or in an email there's usually a better way to say it.

Week 9   **Complaints – a chance to shine!** Be watchful during this session to keep it upbeat and avoid any kind of blame culture.

Week 10   **It's not what you say** It's week 10 now and you should have the confidence to role-play a little and test out some of the ideas more thoroughly.

Week 11   **Service PR** At this point in your training what are you proud of? Contact your press department with some good news stories about your five star service. Be proud!

Week 12   **Service values** This could be your most challenging week as you may not always feel you can change such a huge organisation. Again focus on what you can do.

Week 13   **Spanners and Heroes** Lots of fun, chaos and learning to be had on this your final week. This exercise can take up to one hour so, if you can, schedule some extra time.

Five star for education

Some of my most exciting work is with education – it's also some of my most challenging. Education and its delivery is going through times of great change and your customers – students, parents, employers, government, etc – have very high demands.

Week 1 **The Service Star**™ Every programme starts here. It's how you know where you are and how you'll know when you're getting better!

Week 2 **Wee Wows**™ An easy concept that gives you some quick wins.

Week 3 **Heads up!** Once you have explored the concept be sure to get the buy-in from everyone involved. Schedule a review in a month.

Week 4 **The emotional bank account** Education differs here as customers could feel they have already 'paid' for their service. This means you often start from a place of withdrawal. Explore what that means.

Week 5 **Systemise routines – personalise exceptions** Ensure you have a few examples up your sleeve to get the discussion started.

Week 6 **RADAR thinking**™ As soon as you have completed this session take massive action to implement your ideas. Remember to schedule your review time in too.

Week 7 **One chance to make a first impression and The distraction of dirt** It can be easy to point out some of the things that are wrong with your team here but instead ask your team to point out who does each of the points well.

I've incorporated the distraction of dirt too, not an easy one to address but a vital one. There will be plenty of people who would like to hand over responsibility in this area to someone else. The secret is to make sure everyone feels like they can make a positive difference.

Week 8   **What's in a smile?** This should provide you with lots of quick wins. I know you want to smile, I know you do smile, but public perception is often different. This is your chance to change that.

Week 9   **Making the mundane marvellous** Especially with young people. Education can seem like a drag (we all know they'll think differently in a few years) so it's important to make each part of the learning process, from enrolment to graduation, interesting, stimulating and enjoyable.

Week 10   **Loyalty 3.0** Education is rarely a one-off transaction; you need loyalty for weeks, months and often years. What will make your learners stay with you? How will you keep them with so many other distractions around?

Week 11   **It's not what you say** It's week 11 now and you should have the confidence to role-play a little and test out some of the ideas more thoroughly.

Week 12   **Service values** This could be your most challenging week as you may not always feel that you can change such large organisations. Again focus on what you can do.

Week 13   **Spanners and Heroes** Lots of fun, chaos and learning to be had on this your final week. This exercise can take up to one hour so, if you can, schedule some extra time.

And finally ...

I said at the start of this book the secret isn't in the knowing, it's in the doing. Ideas are just ideas, doing something with those great ideas is what makes the difference.

Edison didn't just think about the light bulb. He made one. Then he opened a company to produce and distribute them. Some would argue that his greatest success wasn't the invention of the incandescent electric light bulb; it was the gift of light for the masses.

The same can be said of great service. It's not really about the service techniques, it's how those techniques *make people feel*. That's what's really special — and you can do that. You can make people feel better about you, your organisation, even themselves! Isn't that amazing?

But it doesn't happen by accident and it certainly doesn't happen by just reading this book. This book is like the manual for a new vehicle. If you've bought a new car recently, you'll notice that you get two books: a quick guide and a detailed manual. The quick guide is designed to get you started and to be used as an instant reference.

You can use *5 Star Service* in the same way, by taking the basic ideas you've learned and immediately applying them. You do have the option to 'drill-down' and use this book as a more detailed manual. The difference will be in your energy and application. However, the difference in the payback and rewards between each method is vast.

Quick-guide benefits and results:

- Hop in and out. You're busy, so just dive in and test the parts that feel most relevant to you.

- Look for some quick fixes (there are some really impactful ones) and experience an immediate improvement in your customer service offering.

- Share the relevant parts with your colleagues. They can follow your lead and quickly be on the same page.

The 'detailed manual' approach:

- Create a real cultural change in your organisation.
- Use 5 *Star Service* as a manual for your WoW – *Ways of Working*.
- Take a chapter each week and as a team spend 15 minutes looking at how you can best apply the ideas. Measure the impact and results and choose which work best for you.
- Keep a journal of the ideas you've used and the impact they have. Record this information and keep your own account of the best way to make the ideas work for you and your organisation.

Whichever method you choose, I hope that by reading 5 *Star Service* you have become as passionate about customer service as I am.

I don't choose the word *passionate* accidentally.

When you're **passionate** about something you'll always **find a way** to make it happen. Even when people say it can't be done, you'll become even more determined and creative.

Passion will give you energy when others have had enough. Passion for people is what's needed to make the ideas in this book really work. If you haven't caught the bug then I suggest you read this book again!

From the Service Star™ to the realisation that everyone could be your competition, I've given you tools and actions to get results. I know what it's like to work in and run an organisation. It's tough, very tough. But now, more than ever, you need to stand apart from the competition. I've found the best way to do that is through amazing Five Star Service.

It's not easy; if it was, everyone would do it. It's not quick, but anything worthwhile seldom is. It's certainly affordable in material costs but it can be emotionally expensive. Whichever way you look at it, creating Five Star magic moments for the people you meet and serve every day has to be one of the most rewarding things you can do.

I hope that one day I have the opportunity to experience your Five Star Service.

What did you think of this book?

We're really keen to hear from you about this book, so that we can make our publishing even better.

Please log on to the following website and leave us your feedback.

It will only take a few minutes and your thoughts are invaluable to us.

www.pearsoned.co.uk/bookfeedback

Acknowledgements

Thank you!

There are loads of people who give their time and energy to make sure you really enjoy this book.

First of all my brilliant publisher, Eloise Cook, who wanted a new edition of 5 *Star Service*, got the backing from Pearson, then challenged me to create the best edition ever. It's amazing to work with a publisher who focuses more on developing what's right than criticising what's wrong.

Next up it's my writing partner, co-director, best friend and my missus, Christine. Gosh, I could go all soppy now but Christine would just cut it out on the first of her many edits!

Paul East has tirelessly publicised my books for years and is always willing to challenge the status quo, find yet another angle and promote my writing to the world. Thank you, Paul.

Lots of people contributed to this book with stories, ideas and enthusiastic support. Here's a list of folks who spring to mind: Jonathan Raggett, Simon Perkins, Capt. Denny Flanagan, Richard Baker, Peter Williamson, Jerry Hall, Nick Wood, Fred Sirieix, Simon Rogan, Nicholas and Michael Wainwright, Rachael Lee, Bernard Murphy, Cheryl Black, Paul Heery, Brian Stanners, Lisa Robinson, Nigel Shanahan, Santiago Cabré, Richard Nugent, Linda Eastwood, Terry Laybourne and Steve Burke at DECIDE. who created the amazing illustrations.

For this edition I also enlisted a new group of people to help. I called them the 5 *Star Rapid Response Team*. Mainly because I usually gave them 24 hours to suggest an idea, choose between A, B or C and give me some very honest feedback on the project. They are: Sheila Breslin, Rob Pickering, Caroline Christer, Nadine Haschka, Chris Hind, Andree Currie, Stuart Isley, Simon Ball, Lisa Burt, Richard Mills, Lena Potse, Andrew Page, Debbie Homer-Davies, Janie Patterson, Jesica Clarke, Vin Patel, Alethea Silk, Steve Walker, Satvinder Bansal and Sandra Loução. Thank for your encouragement, honesty and invaluable suggestions.

And, of course, thank you to you dear reader, for investing your time and money into 5 *Star Service*. I hope you enjoy reading it as much as I enjoyed writing it.

Enjoyed *5 Star Service?*

Free Bonus Chapters and Extra Resources

If you would like to receive the bonus chapters and extra resources mentioned in this book, simply visit www.MichaelHeppell.com and go to the 'Resources' pages.

Book Michael Heppell to inspire at your next event

Would you like Michael to present to your staff and motivate them to passionately deliver 5 Star Service?

Michael has been described as one of the top speakers on the planet!

His keynote presentations and special events have been enjoyed by audiences around the world.

If you would like to know more about booking Michael to speak to your organisation then contact the Michael Heppell Ltd team:

Tel: UK 08456 733 336
           International +44 1434 688 555
Email: info@michaelheppell.com
Website: www.michaelheppell.com

Contact Michael Heppell

For media enquiries, comments or to contact Michael directly, email

info@michaelheppell.com or call (from the UK) 08456 733 336 (or international) +44 1434 688 555

www.michaelheppell.com

 @MichaelHeppell

 Facebook.com/MichaelHeppellOfficial

Praise for Michael Heppell's books

How to Be Brilliant

'It helps you challenge yourself and made me smile in so many ways – I make a pledge to continue to commit to the suggestions and it has given me a new lease of life in both personal and professional ways.'

Mary Bristow

'I really enjoyed the easy reading style and the optimism it imbues. If you need a kick start to energise yourself into action I recommend this book.'

N. Lewis

'This book really is brilliant, and gives plenty of information, suggestions and resources to help you learn how to be brilliant. Plenty of motivating and mindset improving anecdotes and quotes. I've worked my way through quite a few of these books in recent months and this is one of my favourites.'

Kenny Ring

'I was recommended it three years ago and what I learnt from it I will never forget. It doesn't matter if you want to improve personal life or work life, there will be something that will raise an eyebrow, be relevant and change your life forever. I have continued to read it at the beginning of every year since I first read it and I'm sure I will continue to for many years to come.'

Karen Polston

Flip It

'I've read loads of self help books . . . this is the simplest, this is the best.'

Chris Evans, BBC Radio 2

'Best alarm clock I've ever owned, I can't wait to get up in the morning and start to Flip It.'

June Saville

'Can't recommend this book highly enough! Great strategies for positive thinking, already successfully tried at work today.'

Helen Carr

'Heard this book being reviewed on the radio while stuck in a traffic jam and thought it excellent to inspire several members of the family who lack confidence...bought four and they have been invaluable! Would recommend this author for his way of putting words down which are easy to understand and apply to all at some time in their lives.

A great read!'

Yve Blyth

'I would recommend to anyone wrestling with negative thoughts on any situation. This book will arm you with the skills to turn this around.'

Mr D. A. Coleman

'This book is an easy to follow, easy to read, useful tool for turning things from negatives to positives. Easy to learn, digest and make automatic.'

Lynda May

'*Flip It* is different. It's simple, down-to-earth, fun and far more motivating than most of its competition.'

Rob Collins

HOW TO
SAVE AN
HOUR EVERY DAY

GUARANTEED

MICHAEL HEPPELL

How to Save an Hour Every Day

'There are a number of genuinely useful ideas here – either practical "do this" type stuff, or good models that you can apply or that frame your thinking – not just one really good one with 100 pages of additional fluff.'

Len Bappin

'After reading it, I have to admit, I think it probably is possible! Even with a very busy and long working day, there are some great suggestions to organising your life and work, and it is simply a case of finding the ones that work for you.'

Mr S P Lockyer

'So your challenge is equally simple – if you know of someone who fits into the "far too busy for life" category, do them a favour and buy this book, it's Brilliant and they'll love you for it.'

Malcolm Kyle

'. . .this is a clever, easy to read and fun packed book. I laughed out loud with some of the descriptions. There's plenty of tools here to help you to save your hour, or more, every day.'

But for me the book was worth buying for the first sentence – it's genius.'

Linda Lockhart

Brilliant Life

'This is a book EVERYONE needs to read. Not once. Have it by your bed and go back to it for snippets! There's no better gift you could give yourself. Go on! You deserve it!'

Davina McCall, TV Presenter

'A well-written, compelling guide to analysing where we are now, with all aspects of our lives, and where we might want to get to. Altogether a brilliant book that I have already read twice, and do not intend to give away.'

Claire Yell

'This book is awesome, life changing material. You can't just read it once and make a judgement, you have to think about it for a while, work it through then read it again. Then you will find even more important stuff that you missed the first time round. It will happen again and again, every time you read it.'

Mike Haughton

'One of the most accessible and logical to implement personal development books I've read and the only one that has really struck a chord and inspired me to make real, lasting changes.'

Gavin McMurray

'I have read many personal development and coaching related books over the years and this ranks as one of my very favourites. It has a fantastic balance of plain language and simple to understand tools and very powerful and effective exercises tips and techniques.'

Richard Nugent